All Our Yesterdays

The 1930s & '40s
The Depression and World War II

Growing up in Jacksonville, Atlanta, Columbia, and Tampa

Avery Chenoweth, Sr.

Ownership of all publishing, reproduction and copyrights is held by PPP&K/B Inc., under the tradmark of

DISCLAIMER:

As this book is autographical, I do name actual persons whom I have known. I do so in utmost respect and fondness, as they were friends or acquaintences with whom I shared many cherished memories.

In a few cases, I mention a name of which I still have an unfavorable opinion, but I express my own opinion based only on my experiences with that person.

All Our Yesterdays

The 1930s and '40s
The Depression and World War II

Growing up in
Jacksonville, Atlanta,
Columbia, and Tampa

by

Horace Avery Chenoweth, Sr.

Publisher: PPP&K/B Inc.

ISBN: 978-0-9846883-3-3

Cover art by the author

Dedication

To the memory of my dear departed grandparents, Horace Cameron "Daddy Avery" Avery and Rebecca *Reba* Maxwell "Big Buddy" Avery who gave me such a wonderful up-bringing and their generosity in sending me to The Bolles (military prep) School in Jacksonville, and following that, to Princeton University; and to my dear departed parents: Henry Poyntz "Daddy Chick" Chenoweth and Annalee Avery "Little Buddy" Chenoweth, who did their best to raise me and my sister in often difficult times.

No one could have had a better childhood than I.

Avery

Chenoweth

Wales/Cornwall: Trevelesek c. A.D. 700
Chez-Nous/Chenouth/Chenoweth: A.D. 1066
Baltimore, Maryland c. A.D. 1700

Maxwell

Scotland: Prior to A.D. 1250
New York City, A.D. 1680

Faithful • Lose Honor rather than Betray a Trust • I'll Flourish Again

"Big Buddy"
Reba Maxwell Avery
1881-1970

"Daddy Avery"
Horace Cameron Avery
1874-1957

"Daddy Chick"
Henry Poyntz Chenoweth
1900-1969

"Little Buddy"
Annalee Avery Chenoweth
1905-1999

Contents

The 1940s

Tomorrow, and tomorrow, and tomorrow,
Creeps in this petty pace from day to day,
To the last syllable of recorded time;
And all our yesterdays have lighted fools
The way to dusty death. Out, out, brief candle!
Life's but a walking shadow, a poor player
That struts and frets his hour upon the stage
And then is heard no more. It is a tale
Told by an idiot, full of sound and fury
Signifying nothing.

— Macbeth (Act 5, Scene 5, lines 17-28)

Preface

I suppose everyone when he or she reaches old age looks back on former times ... their childhoods especially ... the times they have lived through, with rose-colored memories, particularly in such troubled times as the present. Count me as one of these: not unique, nor with any particular wisdom, didacticism, redemption-seeking, nor just nostalgia for nostalgia's sake, but to leave some sort of record of what some of the now-lost details of life were back then.

My youthful memories are mostly of quieter times...of wondrous things discovered...of a tranquil world that every day offered something new with my changing perspective as I grew. Quite naturally, my perspective (if I could have discerned that back then) was from a low vantage point and extended only as far as I could detect my environment; consequently, everything—as everyone experiences—looked big to me. The places where I grew up are still there—seemingly having shrunk vastly in size from my earlier memories—but most appearing not to have even a single blade of grass changed in over 80 years. Those trees—well, not all—are mostly still there, as are the streets, the sidewalks and the rural and suburban streets. But, gone are the charms of downtowns of yesteryears now buried under intertwining overpasses and towering glass-skinned sky-scrapers.

When I walk down some of those once-familiar streets trying to resurrect some of those childhood experiences, they do come back... some vividly, others faintly. I can, though, almost create the 'spell' of the time past that I was so consciously absorbed in.

So, that is what I will be trying to do in this account of my 'remembrance of times past'. Not to prove I was this or that but merely to convey the ambience of what as a child I experienced back six and seven decades ago, and of the small, now forgotten-details of life in simpler times by painting word pictures of my world through my adolescent eyes as I recall them from the 1930s and '40s.

As occurs to all of us, I suppose, my childhood flash-backs are brief and disconnected. I associate them, therefore, mostly by what grade in school I recall I was at the time. This will explain my departure from a traditional chronological thematic line as my memories come back to me randomly.

Mercifully, I was unencumbered then by knowledge.

"Don't blame all this on me—I just got here!"

The 1930s

The Depression Years

Background:

My first dozen years were, obviously, during this third decade of the 20th Century. What I knew of the times was very little, yet the decade was formative. Those of you who are in your eighties like I am may feel the same way; you younger readers no doubt simply have read books, seen pictures, and heard tell of that period and have ignored it as more or less insignificant.

I only knew from talk that it was a time of Depression, which I surmised meant trouble of some sort. Nevertheless, I found the events and things in that dimly remembered world that touched me, fascinating. Funny, there are occasional black & white photographs of family members but very few of friends—at least of me and my playmates. Photography was fairly common with the Kodak "Brownie" box amateur and the slightly more advanced Kodak bellows type. But a roll of film and its processing cost a good amount for those days and the technical results were a bit iffy. Many are now very faded due to lack of proper washing off of developing chemicals. If one or two shots out of twelve turned out to be good, that was acceptable.

One very particular thing that brings back fond memories is the present nostalgic viewing of the motion pictures of the '30s that can be seen regularly on the Turner Classic Movie (TCM) TV channel. The best films of that period were in hindsight quite remarkable—*remarkable* because the relatively new medium of cinematography had just developed past its infancy, acquiring sound in 1927 that ended the

"Silent Movie Era," but also new filming techniques were quickly perfected instead of the former one of filming as if viewing a stage play. From the first rather good sound movie, Vaudeville singer Al Jolson's "Black-faced" performance in the "Jazz Singer," to "The Singing Marine" to "Snow White and the Seven Dwarfs" to "The Wizard of Oz" and "Gone With the Wind," hardly any motion picture has since surpassed the technique, the dialogue, or the creativity developed during this overlooked decade.

Movies during the Depression era were deliberately aimed at creating "Escapism," of taking people's minds off their miseries. They featured lavish and spectacular musicals and dance routines, sumptuous wealth, white-tie-and tails à la Fred Astaire and his gorgeous dancing partners, Joan Crawford, Ginger rogers, and Rita Hayworth. This, in part, was to divert the public from unemployment, bread lines, and the oft-repeated line of the song: "Brother, can you spare a dime?"—which try as he might, Franklin D. Roosevelt, the new president's adoption of "Happy Days Are Here Again," failed to quell.

After all, that is what *Entertainment* is all about. To lift one's spirits from the mundane. Those sorts of films also embedded themselves in a young impressionable fellow you are about to meet.

Many other significant things in the arts were achieved then: by this decade photogravure printing presses could produce color and fast and continuous Web presses could turn out thousands of copies in just hours. Magazines became a dominant information source and the field of art illustration rose to its zenith in such publications as "The Saturday Evening Post," "Colliers," "Look," "Good Housekeeping," "Vogue," "Time," "The New Yorker," "Liberty," "Popular Mechanics," and a host of others. "Life" magazine debuted in 1936 and, with its predominantly picture format, led the pack and had a profound impact on photojournalism.

Magazine publication had a monetary impact on artist-illustrators —who became very famous and prosperous during tight times: Norman Rockwell was best known, mostly from his humorous "Saturday Evening Post" covers. His delightful works spanned over half of the 20th Century and were unequaled masterpieces of visual chronology of each decade. Ignored by the snobbish, élite art *cognoscenti* as too plebeian, he should be recognized as being in a league with past painters like Bruegel, Bosch, Hogarth, and many others—and, better, too. Rockwell marvelously captured everyday life in a humorous way.

Popular music had come a long way from 19th Century Strauss Waltzes and Stephen Foster songs. At the turn of the 20th Century a negro self-taught genius, Eubie Blake, created a fascinating contrapuntal rhythm in his immortal "Rag Time" tunes that no doubt influenced the subsequent evolution of "Jazz" with its improvised individual melodic harmonies from several instruments simultaneously. Musical operettas were in vogue, such as Kurt Weill's "Three-penny Opera," Victor Herbert's "Babes in Toyland" and "Sweethearts," which were made into motion pictures in the 1930s. And, on the more classical side, Ferde Grofé's "Grand Canyon Suite" with its catchy "Donkey Serenade" that delighted everyone. Or, George Gershwin's earlier great symphonic-jazz piece, "Rhapsody in Blue," that has become a symphonic staple and his American opera, "Porgy and Bess," that had people everywhere humming its "Somertime."

The Fine Arts had been rousted out of its stagnating 'academic' mode by the end-of-the-19th Century rebellion of the European artists of the so-called "Impressionist," "Expressionist," "Cubist," and subsequent "Fauves" (wild beasts), "Surrealist," "Dada," and various spin-off movements that challenged traditional "Realism." "Realism" was not abandoned, though. The marvelous American "Ash Can," and "Regional" artists Sloan, Bellows, Thomas Hart Benton, Marsh, Wyeth, *et al.* stuck to their guns—or *brushes*. During the Depression period, when so many 'fine artists' were out of work, the U.S. government inaugurated a program to help them; under the NRA (the National Recovery Act that was later struck down by the Supreme Court) and the WPA (Works Progress Administration), artists were subsidized with monthly stipends of $41.25 and their work was collected by the government for display. When I was seven or eight, I had studied briefly in Tampa on Saturday mornings in one of the WPA-sponsored art classes for kids.

Two of my own Abstract Ex-Im-Pressionist paintings I did for my MFA at the Univ. of Florida in 1956- '57: Swamp Night *and* Box Bauble.

On the world scene things were turbulent

In my little hemispheric bubble, it was simply a wonderful time to grow up in, despite the far-distant and dismal world scene. "The Great War" (It was obviously not yet being called World War I) had only been over for a dozen years, but in those years the world had changed drastically. Millions had died in the war and millions more in the following influenza epidemic that coursed throughout the world.

The loser of that war, Germany, which like each of the European Allies, had lost a whole generation of its young men and had suffered mightily, declining both economically and financially. Thus civil unrest, the deflation of its currency, and widespread malaise led to Kaiser Wilhelm's stepping down in 1932 and relinquishing the Chancellorship of Germany to an enigmatic, un-educated, rising unknown, Adolf Hitler. Russia, that had pulled out of the Allied side in the middle of the Great War because of internal revolution, succumbed to communism and to ruthless dictatorships, the worst being Josef Stalin, then in power, who proceeded not only to kill off the intelligentsia of his ruthless Communist government but to starve 35 million citizens in his affiliated (Soviet) Ukraine as well.

Concurrently, Italian dictator, Benito Mussolini, gained power and instituted a stern Fascist rule, despite placating the people by "making the trains run on time." His vision of himself as a reincarnate Roman Emperor prompted him to send his army into Africa to cowardly subdue helpless and destitute Ethiopia. Mussolini and Hitler then made an "Axis-Pact" and the set-up for a second World War was irrevocable.

On the other side of the world, Imperial Japan was on the rampage of territorial expansion. Having annexed Korea in 1910, in the 1930's it began rebuilding for war, callously discarding its treaty with Britain and France (through the impotent new League of Nations formed following the Great World War) and proceeding to build up its navy and army. Then, in mid-decade, it set out on its military conquest of Manchuria and China.

In the meantime, in 1936, a civil war occurred in Spain. There, the revolutionaries against dictator Francisco Franco were aided by communist Russia, while Franco was aided by Germany—now under NAZI (National-Socialism) dictatorship. Both sides used the little war to test their armaments, the Nazis notoriously using their newly built Stuka dive bombers to level little Spanish villages like helpless Guernica—a dastardly feat that aroused international anger.

England saw what was coming and started preparing; the French might have, too, but—to their everlasting regret—procrastinated. In 1939, English emissary, Sir Neville Chamberlain, met face-to-face with Herr Hitler to negotiate a halt to Germany's annexation (*Der Anschluss)* of Austria and the German-speaking Sudetenland that lay between Germany and Czechoslovakia. The upshot was Hitlers' deceiving the naïve diplomat who then announced back in the English Parliament: "There will be peace in our time." Within months, on September 1, 1939, Germany invaded neighboring Poland and what would become the Second World War began. After conquering Poland, Hitler forced France to surrender, then turned toward England; in a better territorial position as an island and with a firmer will, the Brits won the aerial Battle of Britain that halted the vicious German bombing of its cities and any possibility of a German invasion. Unable to subdue the English, Hitler then turned and invaded Russia (the Soviet Union), in what was to be the beginning of his downfall.

In America

The 1929 Wall Street stock market collapse had resounding effects as the values of investors' stocks and savings earned from the preceding 'Boom" of the 1920s suddenly plummeted: banks and factories and businesses closed, people lost their jobs, some businessmen jumped out of their office windows, others—now destitute —joined bread lines or sold apples on the street corners. For many, faith in the American system for the most part evaporated; they feared that the Constitutional Free-Enterprise system had failed and that possibly socialism or even communism were better. That heresy was no more insidiously portrayed than in author John Steinbeck's novel of the times, "The Grapes of Wrath." He depicted the plight of the poor farmer of the drought-ridden mid-west in the now destitute "Dust Bowl" that had subsumed formerly fertile farm land—leaving poor families like the literary Joads, clad in their dusty overalls and rags, with no hope but to move to greener pastures—loading their broken-down jalopy (car) and heading for California. They find their solution in coming upon a socialist-communist community (misrepresented by literary critics as a benign U.S. government facility) which, of course, becomes their 'promised land'. None of the plethora of prizes the author won for the book—or the subsequent film in 1939-40—alluded to this flat-out subversive dénouement. The Joads did epitomize the disenfranchised worker of the era—as I write about in the following first chapter.

As to race relations: there was absolute segregation until the end of the coming war—and that's simply the way it was and was the accepted status quo by both whites and negroes. Both races coexisted, if not in harmony, in stand-offish mutual respect—obligatory on the part of the negroes who had no choice but to look to the whites as their benefactors—at least in the South. They might have hated our guts but knew their livelihoods depended on us. They had their pride as well; they dressed like the white folks—because that was the norm. And, they took pride in their churches and in their families—poor as they might be. Their families stayed together; there was very little out-of-wedlock parenting in either of the two communities. Both the mores and morals of society were a common bond.

Society in general was genteel—no overt cursing, not even words commonplace now like 'damn' and 'hell'. The utter vulgarities that were unutterable, like our ubiquitous "F-," "S-," "N-," etc. were scarcely—if ever heard in polite company. When Rhett Butler (actor Clark Gable) uttered those crushing words in Gone With the Wind, "Frankly, (Scarlet) my dear, I don't give a ***damn***," the world was aghast! That became the heated topic of conversation all over the United States (perhaps not so much in Europe). Good old words, too, like "gay" and "rainbow" meant beautiful things back then long before they were corrupted by the homosexual crowd. There was a very naughty pornographic film always bandied about but never seen, titled "The Gay Count." The Count's version of *gay* was a far sight from today's perverted meaning.

None of this penetrated my little mind during that decade, although I sensed some of it. There were rumblings that the inevitable war in Europe was none of America's business and that we should not get involved. It was a period of innocence and apathy—at least to most people. Little did they suspect what that would portend.

So, this is the sort of world that was transpiring unbeknownst to a kid growing up during the time in Jacksonville, Atlanta, Columbia, and Tampa—not at all affecting the sublime happiness of his childhood.

The author in 1933

Horace C. & Reba M. AVERY
with Annalee and Jack
at 624 Lomax St., Jacksonville, c. 1907

Prelude

Inauspicious beginning

My entrance into this world was on July 29th, 1928, precisely at 6:20 PM, a squawking jaundiced-thing in St. Vincent's Hospital in Jacksonville, Florida; that's what the birth certificate says ... and what I was told later. That moment when I took my first breath occurred in the cosmos at the conjunction of Leo and my rising sign of Capricorn. Due to that or some DNA quirk, I was blessed with an almost photographic visual memory—but thank god it kicked in *after* delivery!

That inauspicious year 1928 was between Charles Lindbergh's astounding, at the time, solo flight across the Atlantic ocean to Paris in 1927—the first ever—and the Wall Street stock market crash of 1929 that affected everyone and sent the world reeling.

Neither of these events really affected me, of course...except the latter, perhaps, because it influenced a decade that was most formative in my life: the Great Depression of the 1930s. But to my tiny eyes the world would be just one big wondrous thing all around me, every detail of which would intrigue me, and as I matured I would relish finding out about the 1940s—the war and college years. Those were still relatively simple times but were to hold far more excitement than I ever could have expected.

I was four when my sister Catherine was born,
seen here held by my Daddy Chick

Chapter 1

"When I was in knee-pants..."

I sat myself down on the edge of the back porch next to the strange man who had rung the bell at the front door and who was now seated resting his arms on the tops of his long legs that reached down two steps farther than mine.

I always liked to sit there and look down over the back yard and at the big round tin tub with the steaming water bubbling in it resting on the bricks circling the charcoal fire that blackened its bottom, as Sally the maid poked and stirred the clothes and from time to time raised a heap up on the white bottom of the laundry pole to turn them over...that somehow mesmerized me. But she wasn't doing that now.

As I put my tiny feet with my scuffed sandals on the top step, I looked up at the man and he turned and gave me a vacant look.

Alzonia, the cook, let the screen door slam behind her as she came out of the kitchen and handed the man a kitchen knife and fork and a large dinner plate filled with food...some meat, rice 'n gravy, string beans, cornbread, butter, it looked like...that was hot and smelled real yummy...which he perched on his long lanky lap and began to dig into. She put a tall glass of milk on the floor next to him. He gulped the food like he was really hungry—which he must have been...he was so skinny. He didn't eat like my "Big Buddy" or "Little Buddy"...he was sloppy...and hunched over and his cheeks puffed out as he stuffed more and more food into his mouth with grunt-like noises. He stopped chewing every now and then to take a swig or two of the milk to wash it all down.

He smelled kind a funny and the lower part of his face was all dirty with hair, too. I didn't like it. My "Daddy Avery" and "Daddy Chick" didn't smell like that. And his clothes were dirty. "Little Buddy" would never have let me wear such stinky clothes. He had on soiled overalls and a dingy blue shirt with a dirty crumpled collar. I thought he needed a bath.

> I called my grandfather "Daddy Avery" and my grandmother "Big Buddy." I called them that because I thought I had two fathers, the big one "Daddy Avery" and the slimmer one, "Daddy Chick," and two mothers. Since I couldn't pronounce "mother" and my grandmother was larger than by mother, she became to me, "Big Buddy"—therefore, my mother became "Little Buddy."

The front doorbell had rung and I had followed behind Sally as she opened the door, nodded to the man who humbly asked for just something to eat—didn't matter—to come around back.

As we sat together—this poor soul...silently wolfing this serendipitous repast (as I came to call it later)...I stared at him in awe, I guess that was what it was. Later, more such men would come knocking on the door and would be given something to eat. I wondered why? We always had food to eat...why didn't they? And where were their wives and their children like me? Did they have to go to someone's door and ask for food, too?

The fascinating back yard

Daddy Avery's and Big Buddy's back porch—where we were sitting —and the back yard were places where I didn't go very often. That big back porch was enclosed with a word I heard everybody use: lattice. The lattice seemed to be thin angled strips of wood nailed together criss-crossed covering the two open sides of the porch. And the back door which swung closed where we were sitting was even latticed with all their little diamond-shaped holes that let in the outside air and kept the rain out. It made it a little dark sometimes and I didn't like that, although the back stairs that the lattice also enclosed were the quickest way to get from one floor to another, and the maids always used it.

Under those stairs was the servants' toilet and wash basin. I never went near that.

The back yard was not a good playground. There were only clumps of long funny-looking grass (centipede) that my grandmother chided me for liking to pull up occasionally, and her small garden plots lining the wire fence. The rest was just plain dirt, fine gray dirt...not loose but packed down by feet. Feet coming and going, deliveries being made, the servants entering and leaving the house and the maid tramping all around the big round tin tub set on the bricks where the charcoal fire heated the wash water in it to do the clothes. All our clothes, back then, were heaped and thrown into the boiling water—I suppose it was boiling—some vapor always rose up from it, and then stirred with some sort of soap compound by the servant, Sally usually, who wielded the short bleached pole that had turned bluish and slippery on the end from the heat and the "bluing" from the soap. She'd stand there in the hot sun and stir and dip and turn some heap over and poke and poke and lean back and wipe her brow then let the whole thing simmer some more.

When the precise time for that ended—as only she seemed to know —she would grab some and dip them up and down into another tub of fresh water then put them on a wooden table next to the tub and begin feeding and cranking each item through the twin rollers of the squeezer attached to the table that did its job of ringing them out pretty well.

She followed that by taking that bundle in a basket over to the clothes line. I guess the smaller thin things went onto the upside-down umbrella-like rack that turned around on its main pole. She held some of the shirts, underwear, socks, and other stuff over her arm as she went along picking one to flap out and attach with wooden clothes-pins to one of the five or six taut lines. When she was done with this, she'd take the heavier things, like sheets, and table cloths, and bulky garments—rinse and squeeze them—and take them over to the four straight, higher lines that stretched between two "T-shaped" poles on each side of the yard and again fasten them with clothes pins. From my perch sitting on the top step of the porch it always looked like a bunch of tiny birds resting on the wires. The wires were metal and sometimes when there was a slight breeze they sounded like they were humming.

That fenced-in back yard was a constant source of fascination though, as I pointed out, I did not play in it. Other than my grandmother's small garden plots the whole thing was mostly that gray dirt, like in the driveway and in the one-car garage. The big tin tub always sat on the bricks awaiting a fire underneath for the laundry's weekly boiling. It was there, too, that every Thanksgiving the cook's husband would come over with a large, live turkey—and a heavy axe. He'd grab that big, squawking critter and somehow get its neck on the tree stump chopping block and—**WHAP!**—off would come the head— and off would go the headless body running full tilt around the backyard with its wings flapping and its neck spurting blood until it suddenly dropped dead. Then, the feathers would be plucked off, the carcass stuffed and put in the oven, and by the time I tasted the delicious cooked turkey with all the trimmings, all previous thoughts of how it got there were mercifully forgotten. Back then all the poultry, even that bought at the store, had to be plucked before cooking. Refrigeration was simply great big blocks of ice put in the "Ice Box" in the kitchen or pantry. (I still call our refrigerator the "Ice Box"). A creaky old red mule-drawn wagon driven by an ol' "Darky," as they were called then, would plod around every few days with a load of big blocks of ice kept cooled under a tarpaulin and we kids would run after it and grab ice chips that remained when he grappled an ice block with his big hook and shoulder it and take up to the house and deposit in the Ice Box in the kitchen. Those chips were a wonderful treat for us in the summer heat.

The daily routine

The milkman would park his truck down the street, pack his wire basket with bottles of milk, then walk to the front doors of his customers and deposit the two, of so, bottles of milk on the front doorstep early every morning and pick up the empty ones from the previous day (back then, all glass bottles like milk, Coca Cola, and NeHi soft drinks were returned, sterilized, refilled, and resold. I think you got a penny each for returned Coke bottles). The milk was in glass bottles with little cardboard seals on top. The cream in the big bottle had always risen to the top and was a different color from the rest of the milk; the little bottle was all cream, for the coffee and cereal. I remember later discussions about 'pasteurization'..."Little Buddy" always made sure the milk delivered or that she bought in the market was *pasteurized* because back then a horrible disease called undulant fever came from raw, unpasteurized milk, possibly from the smaller, local farms that sold their small quantities of fresh raw milk themselves. Antibiotics or sulfa drugs were non-existent and scourges like measles, whooping cough, chicken pox, tetanus (Lock-Jaw and septicemia), and dreaded influenza that had killed millions in Europe and the U.S. following the First World War were devastating. (By the 1940s, life-saving antibiotics like Sulfa and Penicillin had been developed)

"Polio" (Poliomyelitis) was rightly feared, too, causing lung paralysis with patients (mostly children) ending up confined to living lying on their backs in an "Iron Lung," an artificial breathing machine. Even President Roosevelt had succumbed to the disease as a young man, losing control of his legs so thus was confined to a wheel chair for the rest of his life. Many—like my mother—thought his polio had resulted from his having stayed too long in a wet bathing suit (men wore bathing 'suits', not trunks, back then), consequently, she was ever vigilant whenever either my sister or I came out of a swimming pool or the ocean to make sure we changed to dry clothes. (To the great benefit of all mankind, a vaccine against polio was discovered in 1950 that eradicated the disease.)

I had begun to hear talk about the "Depression," which I had no idea what that meant except that a lot of people were out of work and suffering—like the poor men who came to our door begging for food. So it was no surprise when an occasional boarder would be taken in by my grandparents, too; a working man who would rent a bedroom and go up the street to Five Points where the shops to eat were and take the streetcar to work downtown. There were numerous 'Boarding Houses' near the downtown area which were where young single working men found convenient domicile, as meals were served as well—a tradition of long standing soon to be replaced after the coming war by apartments and motels. The Averys' home was not a real boarding house but they simply took in friends of friends who were in need—and no meals were offered to the boarders.

A trivial thing I will never forget was the distant haunting sound of the train whistle that I heard especially in the early dawn before I got up or long after I had gone to bed. Up through the war and well into the 1950s railroads were predominant. They connected to everywhere anyone wanted to go and were the only way to really travel long distances as there was then no major network of roads connecting every city, town, village, and hamlet—much less airlines. Going to summer camp—Camp Carolina—in North Carolina in 1943 was via train—a real "choo-choo" train with coal smoke chugging and puffing and coming in through some of the open windows and causing us captured passengers to cough and squint—much less try to nap.

The newsboys delivered the *Florida Times-Union* in the mornings and the *Jacksonville Journal* in the late afternoon. If there was a big special news event, the newspapers would quickly print an "Extra" edition that would be hawked by newsboys on the sidewalks downtown for the business people. The mailman also brought the mail to us twice a day, walking door-to-door hunched slightly away from the shoulder over which the thick leather strap supported the very large heavy leather sack that held all the mail which he dutifully deposited in the slots in the front doors—or laid on the porch.

The Sunday morning newspaper was the most anticipated because there were a lot more comic strip pages (we called them 'funny papers') and they were often in color. I'd spend a whole day (there was no nursery or Kindergarten Sunday School then) down on the floor pouring over each one of them...over and over. Of course, there was "Popeye, Olive Oyl, and Wimpy" and "Maggie and Jiggs" (actually "Bringing up Father"), "Dick Tracy," "Little Orphan Annie," with Daddy Warbucks, and the dog, Sandy, "Dagwood and Blondie," and one that always fascinated me because I could never figure where they were supposed to be: "The Katzenjammer Kids" (South Africa, someone said —wherever that was). Later came "L'il Abner," "Flash Gordon," "Tarzan," "Terry and the Pirates," and "Smilin' Jack." I absorbed every one of them and when they came out in comic-book form or "Big-Little

Books," I began collecting them, adding "Superman," "Red Ryder," "The Lone Ranger," and others.

Later during the war, the cartoon "Smilin' Jack" fascinated me because creator Zack Mosley used German phrases in his strips which I tried to memorize. Bobby Davis, my next door neighbor on River Road when we moved to the Southside and I attended Bolles military academy together; he knew Mosley and was good enough to have the artist draw this for me—which I still have:

The H.C. AVERY house at 624 Lomax St., built in 1903
The near porch corner was enclosed and a rear 2nd floor Sleeping Porch was added in 1938

My grandparents, the Averys, lived about a mile and a half south of downtown Jacksonville on Lomax Street where it crosses Riverside Avenue that parallels the St. Johns River. My formative years were progressively in Jacksonville, Atlanta, Columbia SC, Tampa, and back to Jacksonville in between and every summer. They covered the entire Great Depression of the 1930s, during which my family suffered little due to my grandfather's owning and running a large warehouse business (The Union Terminal Warehouse and Cartage Co.) and my Dad's job as a claims adjuster for the Firemen's Fund Insurance Agency.

Wherever we were living...Atlanta, Columbia, or Tampa...my sister and I were always sent back to Jacksonville to spend the summers here with grand Daddy Avery and Big Buddy. The house still stands today, although as a commercial entity in need of much repair.

CHAPTER 2

The Big House on Lomax St.

The Inner Sanctum

From the back porch where we were sitting to get into the house you had to go through the kitchen. The kitchen always smelled good but was large and dark with the ice box right inside beside the door next to the sink under the only window and farther, the dark, dank pantry with its rows of shelves with cans of stuff and little bottles and pots and pans. The big iron hooded stove (it wasn't wood-burning so it must have been electric) dominated the opposite wall and there was a table and a chair on the wall next to it where the food was prepared by the cook and put on plates for the maid to serve the family at mealtimes. The chair was for the either of them to eat at or rest in every now and then.

Off the kitchen where some more preparation was done for the meals was a little hallway that opened with a swinging door into the big dinning room with its big, heavy octagon-shaped table where we all sat for meals—me usually on a telephone book and my sister in a high chair. Behind the table on the wall that separated the living room was another fireplace...probably in back of the one in the living room, but I never remember a fire in it. Along the side wall was a big (everything was Big, of course) cabinet on tall, thick legs where the silver forks, spoons, and knives were kept as well as the silver trays and pitchers and goblets and fancy tea pots. (The servants polished them all the time) Above this furniture was a row of small windows that also had pretty colored glass in them. (Tiffany glass)

If you came into the big house instead from the sidewalk in the front, you had to climb the wide front steps up to the big front porch that went around one side of the house with its thick round columns holding up its roof. The front door was big—everything was all so "Big" to me, of course—dark wood with an oval glass window covered by a thin curtain on the inside. Right inside the door to the right was the first landing of the staircase going up to the second floor and it had a small round window with colored glass so when the sunlight shone through it, it looked pretty but you couldn't see anything through it; it was too high up for me to look, anyway. There was a framed picture on the wall in another room of my mother, "Little Buddy," in her long white wedding dress posed standing on the landing in 1927, the year before I was born.

The living room was big and there was a big fireplace in the center. It was a dark room with heavy curtains and big chairs and two sofas and a big Persian rug on the floor. **Big, big...big**! Everything! I had to climb up onto everything

If you went straight from the front door to the far adjoining room, the "study," you would pass over a large iron grate flat in the floor that looked like a big waffle iron. That was where the heat from the furnace came up on cold days. It was full of holes naturally and it always scared me to peek down into the darkness below wondering what would happen to me if I fell into it—and I was very careful not to let any of my tiny toys, especially toy cars, roll close to it. The fire must have been down there but I couldn't see it—it was always dark. But I knew there was a fire down there because my Daddy Avery would sometimes let me go with him down the steps into the basement to watch him open the little door on the furnace to see the fire and how big it was and to stoke it or shovel more lumps of black coal into it. The coal was heaped in a dingy bin of sorts right under a small window which was where the coal was dumped down from the outside whenever a big truck would stop and deliver it. That basement was very mysterious and dirty and certainly I had no urge to play down there. This made the grate on the floor above it all the more ominous; even one time my toddler sister fell on top of it and burned her knee. The iron was not red hot but hot enough to cause a slight waffle-shaped burn. She screamed bloody murder and everybody—mother, dad, the servants—all came scurrying. And, I don't know what they did back then for first aid, probably coated it with butter. Anyway, she got over it alright.

Once I crept past the grate, the study beckoned. It was like a library with lots of books...big picture books, especially of the "Great War" just passed. There were others, too, that I read when I got older and could read. I loved the Tom Swift ones but was a bit puzzled by their odd clothes. Tom's adventures enthralled me nonetheless. One, "Tom Swift in the Land of Volcanos" was particularly fascinating. How could there ever be such a land with a long row of fiery volcanos emitting puffs of smoke? (I was to find out seven decades later when I traveled to Guatemala) And, there was a stack of *National Geographic* magazines; the pictures were in black and white and, of course, the African native women with bare breasts were something to peek at. Whenever I had toys, like at Christmas—and the Christmas tree was always in this room —I would spread them all around, especially the Lionel electric train and its oval track. Many pleasant hours were spent in that room and on that floor.

A not-so-pleasant surprise

One day, that I recall so vividly when I was about four, I was playing in the dirt driveway of DA's and BB's big house when "Little Buddy" and "Daddy Chick"—"Chick" is what his sisters called him so I picked that up and associated it with daddy—came out of the side door and I spotted my pajamas folded in her arms. "Why do you have my pajamas? It's not bedtime."

"No we're just going for a ride... so let's go get in the car."

I dutifully obeyed, wondering what this was all about.

My next recollection was in a long hallway inside the hospital...in my pajamas...and then being put onto something...and then seeing this cup-like thing coming down over my nose...and nothing more—until a day or so later when I was told that I had had my tonsils taken out. I didn't know what that was—except that it was something about my throat—and I felt OK...a little sore... so didn't dwell on it. (I had been given ether, and to this day I think I can still smell it!)

An unforgettable experience

One day when about the same time, Daddy Avery announced that the new president would be driving by up the street and that we should walk up to the corner (of Lomax and Riverside Avenue) and watch him go by.

Anything out of the ordinary was OK with me, so off we went.

And, sure enough, a few minutes later a big car with no top drove slowly by and there was a man with a hat on sitting in the middle of the back seat. My grandfather said, "There goes President Franklin D. Roosevelt!" I must have clapped my little hands or yelled in innocent glee.

Then, Daddy Avery said, "Come on, let's see him again at the other end of the street up at "Five Points."

So, we did and saw him ride by in the big car again, waving at us and all the other people standing on the sidewalk. (That marked the first of all the presidents I have seen personally up through Reagan.)

This is similar to the way I saw President Franklin Delano Roosevelt in 1933 driving by (not, of course), with former President Hoover [left] with him.

*My grandmother and I in 1932 on the steps
of the front porch at 624 Lomax Street*

CHAPTER 3

My Grand Mother: "Big Buddy"

My grandparents always had a cook, a servant, a cleaning woman, and, when my sister and I visited, a nurse—always negroes. We children looked up to them affectionally as guardians, "nannies," and protectors. My grandmother, Rebecca "Reba" Maxwell Avery, affectionately referred to them as "Nigras,"—and treated them as part of the family.

These were, of course, the days of segregation of the races; however, there was a mutual respect of sorts: most whites, like my grandparents and parents and most of the more affluent class treated them well, often almost as members of the family. Modern readers might not like it—but "they knew their place." No doubt their deference was a form of self-preservation in uncertain circumstances. Many negro servants though, especially cooks, stayed with families all their work lives. To us moderns, their pay—usually a few dollars a week—seems exploitive but back then it was as relative as the minimum wage is today. Besides, with no welfare or medicaid, few negroes—or anybody, for that matter —had anywhere to go for dire emergencies except to a hospital—where negroes were treated virtually 'at the back door'. Whites who could afford one usually had a cook, others had an additional maid who did the housework, and, if there were children, another negro nurse who, while the children were in school or during nap times, had to help the maid in household chores. In addition to their weekly pay they were fed the same three meals a day as the family and were often allowed to take left-overs home; furthermore, they were given "car fare" to ride the street car. Of course, in inclement weather, or if feeling 'poorly', they would be driven to their homes on the other side of town.

The Family secret

A "hush-hush" family secret that I only found out from a faded news clipping after my grandmother died in 1970 was that she had been assaulted one evening in 1924 right in the driveway at 624 Lomax as she was getting out of her car, by a negro who thrust her back in and drove out into the countryside, beat her, and dropped her off on the side of the road in the dark. She was in her forties, strong, and despite bleeding and bruised, was able to stumble her way to a distant house for help and was quickly hospitalized. The newspaper article did not give her name—only a 'society woman'—but went into exacting detail about the police and a detective tracking the man, cornering him, and—when he resisted arrest—shot him dead. This was preferable to lynching that might have happened had he killed my grandmother. Anyway, the detective gave his .38-caliber "Police Positive" revolver that he killed the man with to my grandfather, and I have it to this day.

Quite incredibly—although she lost her wonderful soprano voice from damage to her larynx, she never held any animosity toward "Nigras" thereafter, and we had many loyal and affectionate servants.

"Big Buddy" was a large, soft woman...soft of speech and manner... elegant, poised, and very talented. Before I was born she had been a concert singer of some local fame—until the unfortunate episode described above. She probably had more influence on me than anyone else in the family because she was always there...while Daddy Avery was always at work, except on Saturday afternoons and Sundays; the work week back then was Monday through Saturday noon. And, when my sister and I were in Jacksonville that meant that my parents were back wherever we called home at the time.

I never thought of "Big Buddy" as "old"—I had no concept of age beyond either child or adult and between her and my mother, "Little Buddy," only the difference in size. She carried herself with charm and poise and never raised her soft voice. She was very sweet and imposing...regal like a Queen. Her days were tranquil. She ran the household, instructing the Nigras in their chores, overseeing the menus and marketing...the "Piggly Wiggly" grocery store was just up the street a couple of blocks at "Five Points." She had a big car—a Packard, as I recall (Daddy Avery always drove a Chrysler)—and often my sister and I would be allowed to go with her to shop. All the stores back then had a front section where only a small amount of produce or items were displayed for purchase, the rest was stored in the larger room in the back. Free-standing displays had not been invented as yet. Consequently, on busy days 'stock boys' were constantly going back and forth resupplying the dwindling shelves. (It wasn't until after the Second World War that modernization and mass marketing led to more efficient 'front stocking' where most of everything to be bought was distributed on larger shelves in the main store instead of in storage in the back)

After her unfortunate episode that coast her her singing voice, "Big Buddy" turned to poetry and writing and spent her quiet afternoons upstairs in her big 'sitting room' adjacent to the master bedroom with the standing fan slowly swinging back and forth cooling her and wafting aloft the aura of a slight fragrance of perfume that always hung about her...or she, fanning herself with the folding hand fan that was always hanging from a strap on her wrist...as she wrote her poems or read. At a certain time in the afternoon she would turn the radio on and listen to the 'soap operas', like "Ma Perkins" and "Stella Dallas," whose lethargic droning voice I can still hear in my mind. There were other programs she listened to but I usually did not hang around to hear them. I much preferred—as did the whole family—the evening line up of comedy radio programs like "Amos and Andy," "Jack Benny," "Allen's Alley," "Fibber McGee and Molly," and on Saturday evenings, "Your Lucky Strike Hit Parade."

My grandmother became recognized nationally as a poet of the time and had two books published as well as winning several national prizes.

I guessed she was kind of important because of this. One of her many nationally published poems was this little one that touched even me at a tender age by its verbal imagery:

> Lighthouse
> It loomed ahead, through misty air,
> A mammoth silver tree,
> The thousand whirling seagulls there,
> Its silver leaves blown free.

She was also a member of the National Pen Women's Society and was a very active member of the Jacksonville Women's Club, serving as its president a couple of times over the years. As early Jacksonville residents at the turn of the 20th Century, she and Daddy Avery both traced their heritages back to the Revolution in organizations like the "Colonial Dames," "Daughters of the American Revolution" and "Daughters of the Confederacy," and Daddy Avery, the "Sons of the American Revolution," (things that were rather important back then). The "Averys," of course, were in the stratum of Jacksonville "Society" of community leaders. Thus, they were members of the social clubs, the "Timmucuana Country Club" and "Florida Yacht Club" and charter members of the "Ponte Vedra Club" (long before it became *Sawgrass)* south of Jacksonville beach (where they also had a cottage built right on the beach as well). With all this, of course, came the "Debutante" syndrome—the introduction of daughters of the wealthy to Society through the women's "Junior League," virtually to announce the availability of a daughter of marriageable age to the right young man of similar social status. "Little Buddy" had "Debuted" in the mid 1920s. I suppose this was the closest to "class" distinction that existed back then but it did not entail snobbery...it was just an assumed thing...and not "Lorded" over anyone. I thought that's the way all the world was.

In her spacious sitting-room, Big Buddy had a wire bird cage with a canary that chirped and fluttered every now and then. She never let it fly around the room, though. Also, she had two fluffy Persian cats—one white and the other black, which she named "Amos" and "Andy" after that very popular program in those infant days of radio. They were in and out of her lap all the time and lived to be 18 years old. I was very fond of them as they were very docile and soft. The "Amos and Andy" comedy half hour on radio was voiced by two white men carrying on a "Minstrel" tradition of the popular traveling theater from the 19th century known then as "Vaudeville" which were live variety shows that were performed on local stages or in movie theaters along with the feature movie. (I saw one of the last true Vaudeville shows in a movie theater in Tampa in 1936 or '37. I sensed it was a bit raunchy though mostly over my head) Vaudeville singers, dancers, and comics travelled all over the country from city to city performing live on stage after stage. It was an art form in itself and when motion pictures were perfected and sound included after 1927, Vaudeville was a ready-made gold mine of talent that transitioned easily into the movies now being turned out in Hollywood, California: Jack Benny, Bob Hope, Joe Penner, the Marx Brothers, Eddie Cantor, James Cagney, *et al.*

As I mentioned, my grandmother had been a concert singer before she was injured, so had a wide knowledge of music, part of which, quite naturally, was Opera. She no doubt sang some arias—although I was never privileged to hear her sing. I heard much praise from others from time to time who had heard her, especially the Episcopal Church of the Good Shepherd in Avondale, where she was a frequent soloist and where they worshipped. "Daddy Avery" had installed and dedicated a large (**big**) stained glass window in memory of their son, my mother's older brother, Jack, who had died at 15 from lock-jaw as a result of a tetanus infection from a basketball injury (Lock-jaw was a dreaded disease back then as there was no vaccination against it).

Anyway, she had a marvelous collection of terra-cotta-colored 'shellac' 78-rpm records of operatic selections that she played many an afternoon as I lay on the rug with, probably a purring and cuddling Andy (Amos, the black one, was a bit skittish), absorbing the beautiful sounds; this was one of the most precious gifts of all that she ever gave me—a deep and abiding appreciation of music...classical and especially operatic. The Victrola that played the records was a big wind-up type (with a folding crank handle on the side) with a large cornucopia-shaped, megaphone speaker above it. I don't recall but it must have played a good five minutes before winding down, taking with it the high notes and grinding down to a creepy growl.

One aria that was a particular favorite of mine was *Mon coeur s'ouvre à ta voix...* from Camille Saint-Saëns' opera "Sampson and Delilah." It was sung by Amelita Galli-Curci, one of the greatest of operatic sopranos of her time. I was about seven or eight and Big Buddy taught me to pronounce the titles, and I learned the names and heard the voices of Enrico Caruso, Lily Pons, Jan Peerce, Lauritz Melchior, Lawrence Tibbet, Licia Albanese and many others. That was fortified by my parents always listening to the Saturday afternoon radio broadcasts of the "Texaco Metropolitan Opera" from New York City. No matter where—at home or on the radio in the car on an afternoon drive—so, I grew up with Grand Opera (and had more meaningful connections with it later in life). Galli-Curci also sang another one I liked: *Depuis le jour où je me suis donnée...* from Charpentier's "Louise." Instinctively I seemed to understand these, and thus was sown the seed of my later love of languages—and especially my study of French and German (and Spanish) in college—was certainly planted by her as she pronounced these titles for me to learn. My mother and father also had an ear and eye for culture which strengthened mine but it was my grandmother who really instilled it.

> My grandmother was very artistic, musically and literarily, as my mother was somewhat. My father was quite an artist—a frustrated one—by having to squelch that in the Depression to earn a living in insurance—probably that he

detested—since, being on the claims adjusting side did not earn the lucrative commissions those on the sales side did.

As to classical and operatic music, that was balanced by the great "Big Band" music of the times...the Tommy Dorsey, Harry James, Benny Goodman, Glenn Miller, Artie Shaw, and all the other greats. One very popular song was "Lazy Bones...sleeping in the sun...how you speck to get your days work done?" (Johnny Mercer & hoagy Carmichael). Like kids today, I knew all the lyrics. But, the lyrics—the libretti—or operas I began to learn as well...in later years, of course. And in my Junior year at Princeton in 1948, I took advantage of free Metropolitan Opera tickets to Friday night performances and would take the train to New york City and delight in experiencing the greats singing the greats. One time I got so carried away that I asked how I could "BE" in an opera: more of that, later. Reciting French and German operatic arias and poems that I had learned often helped me preserve my sanity during lulls in the fighting in the Korean War.

To this day, my wife's and my life are filled with as much classical music as we can find on public radio and DVDs.

In those days long before television changed lifestyles, cool evenings after the sun went down were often spent sitting on the front porch listening to the night noises and enjoying some respite from the heat. In the front yard between the sidewalk and the street was a large, spreading yellow tree...at least its strange leaves were yellow. They were rows of tiny little yellow petals that I liked to reach up and strip off a stem of them every now and then. The tree was a beautiful Chinese Mimosa—a very unusual one for Jacksonville and people would often drive by the house just to see it and marvel...to my grandparents' delight.

Daddy Avery and Big Buddy would sit—she, now and then snapping open the small Japanese fan attached to her wrist to shoo away a mosquito or two—as they gently rocked back and forth in their wooden rocking chairs with the caned seats and backs. I would get a stool or something and sit with them or roll around on the porch with a toy car. There was little conversation...just the pleasant absorption of the tranquility of the twilight...perhaps watching the fireflies and dragon flies flitting around over the small lawn. Hardly a car passed—there really weren't all that many anyway back then. Some of the day's news might be commented on...or an incident down at the warehouse...or what those dreadful Roosevelts were doing in the White House—especially the First Lady, Eleanor—of whom my grandmother was not particularly fond. I never heard any harsh words, though, nor did I ever hear any curse words from either them or my parents. Vulgarisms were unheard of in those more innocent days. Even "damn" and "hell" were never uttered.

Many a time my grandmother would tell a story or about something interesting to me or my sister. One I particularly remember was that she often said, "Just remember—this, too, will pass." I pondered long on that, but the one I most vividly recall that intrigued me was: "Time flies. We cannot. They pass at irregular intervals." I relished the 'triple-entendre', even though I did not know what that was at the time.

"Big Buddy" as I remember her as I was growing up

Coping with the heat

It was hot most of the time—all year—but it didn't phase me; I simply thought that's the way the world was. There was no such thing as air-conditioning back then. I think there was an attic fan in their big house...at least sometimes the drop-door in the ceiling for the attic ladder was left open I guess to ventilate—but my parents never had one until after World War II. These big fans did at least create a flow of air that afforded some relief. Also, because of the stifling heat and the constant—and greatly appreciated cooling daily rain showers—closing windows all the time was aggravating...so many houses, like my grandparents', had striped canvas awnings over each window so they could be kept open all the time.

I guess it was the mid 1930s when the heat simply got to everybody. Daddy Avery then decided to have a sleeping porch built off the back bedroom right over the back yard. It was done forthwith and spanned the width of the back of the house and was paneled up to mid wall then all screening up to the rafters and ceiling. It was wonderful. Just like camping out. There must have been eight small beds and cots lined up side by side for all the family to sleep there during the stifling summer nights. We could hear all the nighttime chirpings of the crickets, the haunting train whistles in the distance, and many times in the early morning the "rat-tat-tat" of machine gun practice down the river at the Army Camp Foster Johnson, that later became the U.S. Naval Station once the new war started.

A sort of relief came in the later 1930s with some movie theaters advertising being air-conditioned, "70 Degrees Inside!" It was very cool and refreshing when you first went in but now I doubt it was 70 degrees—coming in all hot and sweaty you'd have caught pneumonia.

The "Avery Cottage" on Duval Drive, Jacksonville Beach, Florida

CHAPTER 4

The house at the beach

The beach house just south of Jacksonville Beach on the Atlantic Ocean (considered at the time part of Ponte Vedra) that my grandfather had built in 1934 or '35 became the Mecca and greatest summer attraction of all our childhood. (It cost around $2,500 to build then: my sister sold it in 2004 for $500,000, and it resold, after renovations, for $1.5 million) The house was two stories and all lightly stained wood inside. All the houses were on a long sand dune (now completely grassed) that formed a slight promontory facing the ocean with the street paralleling it in the back. Right behind that was a man-made lagoon that had quite naturally attracted indigenous wildlife. Sometimes a couple of men would drive up during the night towing a row boat, launch it, get in it, turn on a high-powered flashlight—spot two reflections together of a 'gator's eyes—shoot right between them and drag themselves out a 10-foot alligator. When the houses were being built along the dunes, nests of rattle snakes were rousted; no telling how many moccasins were in the lagoon. All of us kids had the good sense not to go near it.

Turning off that back street, the car would drive up the incline to the two-car garage, and somebody would have to get out and heave one side of the two garage doors up, then everyone would pass inside past the showers and half-bath and ascend the three steps and enter through the back door. Once inside, a few more steps took you past the stairs into the living room that faced the ocean through a window and front door that opened onto a wide, screened front porch. (Later, the whole wall was removed and the entire wall was opened up to view the marvelous panorama from the living room.) A brick-faced fireplace stood at the left wall and was welcomed many a wintry might, since there was no central heating.

The door on the front porch was on the right side instead of centered which would have ruined the view. The grassed front lawn matched all the others in the line of houses to the right and left. Here and there were not too tall palmetto palm trees, some clustered together. At the corners of the porch were bunches of Yucca plants which were more commonly called "Spanish Bayonets" due to the long sharp needles at the end of each long, thick green leaf. They were dangerous. One time I had just gotten a little puppy and we took him to the beach house and let him run in the front lawn—tragically, he ran right into one of the sharp points that put one of his eyes out. Poor thing, it suffered terribly—blind, of course, in that eye—and back then there wasn't a vet nearby to go to. I don't remember but I guess we had him put down. After that, my grandmother gave me a pair of scissors and I went around cutting off the harmful points.

That front lawn—as pretty as it was—was hard to keep that way, what with the sandy soil and the breezy salt air constantly permeating everything, including the closets upstairs in the house that were always musty and humid no matter what airing was tried. At one time I remember the whole yard was plowed up and a foot or so of rich black oozy muck from the swamps (that are now the Sawgrass golf course) was spread all over it and reseeded. The grass (again centipede) came back beautifully but had to be watered and cut all the time.

In the off-season or when the family was not using it, the house was rented by the month. Mostly the residents were decent people, that is who could afford the rent and had manners. But, one time I noticed to my horror that a small original oil painting of a ship at sea—one I had admired for years—had disappeared. Yep. One of the tenants had liked it as well and simply took it. The realtor was negligent in not having kept track of the inventory following each rental. I was really ticked off; it was an excellent painting. To me, it was a heartless violation.

The front lawn sloped down to a concrete bulkhead that stood five or so feet above the sand of the beach. The water's edge came up to only about fifty yards of it at high tide and at low tide the beach was over a hundred yards wide of wonderful, soft, white, sparkling sand. We kids—and there were plenty of neighbor kids—spent all our waking hours running, playing, jumping in and out of the surf, building sand castles, and getting burned to a crisp by the sun's rays.

Nobody seemed too worried about sunburn back then; I'd come in for supper red as a lobster and mother would put a wet towel on my back and I'd go right to the dinner table and eat (after, of course, getting out of my wet bathing trunks).

An acrylic painting I did from the front lawn in the 1980s

After supper, everyone would gather to take long walks down the beach to the less populated parts that were just being developed, near what is now the Ponte Vedra Innlet Resort...the soft breezes in the salty air bearing the long lines of low-flying pelicans skimming the wave tops and the squawking swirling seagulls before they all turned in for the night.

The search for sea shells usually didn't yield much but every now and then we'd come across a good conch or star that was perfect. Sharks' teeth were all over the place. One time, after a horrendous North-Easter storm, a part of the beach was eroded and disclosed a long-ago abandoned section of badly rusted railroad track right at the water's edge. It seems that the tiny coquina clam-like shells left behind by spawns of little donax left behind by each fading wave—and one could see them burrowing themselves in the sand—besides providing a tasty salty soup made from the live ones collected by scooping up hands-full of sand and straining them out, their tiny shells made good cement mixtures and walkway pavings, hence the collecting and hauling by a tracked container to awaiting trucks farther down the beach. Occasionally, we'd see some dunces who had driven their automobile into the shallow water of the surf and were washing it— with salt seawater! Even I knew that was stupid. Their cars must have rusted before they got home!

Another thing that was more than stupid—it was sickening—was what some families did upon returning to Jacksonville after a day at the beach. You have to visualize the automobiles of the 1920s and '30s: They were tall, boxy and roomy inside, and outside had running boards on each side that were simply a long step from the bottom end of the front wheel fender all the way to the bottom of the rear wheel fender. You first stepped on that to enter either the front or back seats. In movies of those times cops would be portrayed standing on the running boards holding onto the door frame with one hand and shooting the bad guys with the other as the chase careened down the road. Well, the beach frolickers, who usually after changing from their wet bathing suits inside the car to their dry clothes, would hang the wet ones to dry draped on the windows that were then rolled up tightly to secure them. The horrifying thing, though, was that if they had brought their family dog along for a dip in the ocean, too, they would not let it back inside the car wet—so perched it precariously on the running board for the 25-mile trip back on rough Beach Boulevard...where the poor thing had to try to balance the curves and bumps and not fall off. It saddened one to see that and even more so to see the dead canine carcasses that lined the road.

44

A tragedy occurred on the beach one day: the younger, 5-year-old brother of one of my playmates had been playing near the rope barrier that stretched across the beach to stop automobile traffic for some reason. The boy had been holding onto the rope when a car driven by a drunk driver came careening toward the barrier—and hit the rope the boy was holding—and the rope rasped his thumb and the palm of his hand nearly completely off. People came running to his screams and did their best to wrap his hand—of course in those days there was no EMS like today, nor medical help nearby—only "Life Guards" far up the beach with only rudimentary knowledge of First Aid. His father drove him all the way 25 miles into Jacksonville for emergency treatment, but in those days before real antiseptics and life-saving procedures, loss of blood and tetanus setting in and the poor child had no chance. It shocked us all and there was a hue and cry for stricter ordnances, as you might imagine. It might be hard for modern-day mothers to realize the absolute fear that mothers of those days lived with; so many children—as well as adults—died of so many things that are trivial and easy to cure nowadays.

For minor cuts and bruises, the first remedy was to hold the wound under the water faucet and wash the blood and germs away, then to put either non-stinging red mercurochrome or really stinging iodine...then wrap it. (I think "Band-Aids" had been invented then; I know there was adhesive tape and will tell about that later on.)

When it rained on the beach we would often go out and run in the sand or splash into the surf—n'ary a thought to the danger of lightning striking us. I don't know how we survived. Otherwise, we stayed indoors and played games. Some of the favorites was Parcheesi, Chinese Checkers...with colored marbles that had to progress somehow over a star-shaped playing board...or cards (not bridge or poker)...or "Pick-up-Sticks" or some such. The big radio stood in the corner and I used to turn the dial to short-wave and listen to all sorts of broadcasts (when I could locate a clear channel that cut through the static), especially from Cuba, which in later years when I studied Spanish, I caught some of it on "La Cadena (chain) de las Americas." One time a Cuban boy came to visit for a week. My grandfather had arranged it through his business club, "Rotary." I'll never forget his name: Julio

Caesar Valcárcel. I figured out that from Julio came the word July, and from Caesar Agustus (whom I had somehow heard of) came the month of August; it was only from later study that I made the obvious connection with Julius Caesar. Although we could communicate very little to each other, we had a grand time...even went down below St. Augustine to the newly opened "Sea World Aquarium." This was a marvel of the time and a 'first.' It was incredible to see the sea creatures up close and watch them swim. Much better than have one take a swipe at your leg when wading in shallow water—which did happen—but not to me.

During World War II, incredibly there was a bit of enemy action off Jacksonville Beach a couple of miles down from us. First was the four Nazi saboteurs who landed during the night from a German submarine onto south Ponte Vedra Beach. Four others with the same mission and modus did so in New England. All eight were quickly caught by the FBI, quickly tried, and seven were executed as 'spies' within a couple of months.

In sight of the shore (although I never saw it) on a few nights a German submarine would surface and torpedo a "Liberty Ship" freighter just leaving the mouth of the St. Johns River and past the long granite rock jetty. The sky would be lit up with gunfire and the exploding ship. As a consequence, the entire beach and the entire county and city of Jacksonville were under a nighttime light 'Black-out' restriction those four years of the war. Light-tight window shades had to be drawn and the top half of automobile headlights had to be painted black to dim them. The glow from the city itself 25 miles from the coast and all up and down the U.S. Atlantic coast could silhouette merchant shipping. Volunteer neighborhood "Air Wardens" patrolled to make sure everyone obeyed the restrictions—many at the time thought, too, that the Germans could have bombed the East Coast (which the wiser military did not discourage). Actually, the U.S. West Coast experienced an isolated attack or two from Japanese submarines and once a Japanese incendiary balloon landed in Oregon doing little damage. Of course, the Japanese early on following Pearl Harbor had seized the American Aleutian island of Attu but later abandoned it.

German artist's depiction of a Nazi U-Boat giving the finishing touches to a freighter it has just torpedoed. They never rescued survivors. (Similar to what happened off Jacksonville beach)

Chapter 5

La plus ça change, la plus la même chose

Today, while the Jacksonville Beaches and Ponte Vedra—and the city itself—have grown and changed dramatically, the older neighborhood in Riverside looks pretty much just the same as it always has since the early 20th Century: stately oaks draped with Spanish moss still tower on each side of the street, large houses—some mansions built during the real estate 'boom' of the 1920s—lining it on either side as well, glimpses of the river at cross streets, spacious, "Memorial Park" just beyond Lomax street on the river with a circular sidewalk ideal for roller-skating and a huge intriguing monument of the world out—or off of—which appear to emerge human figures of men, women, and children in varying stages of evolving. This strange universe is the nucleus that towers above a circular pool around which runs a low concrete wall that is ideal for sitting and contemplating the meaning of the fascinating blue-patinated bronze centerpiece. Sometimes people would throw coins into the water—as if it were a "Wishing Well"—and we used to take off our shoes to wade in and fetch some.

The park's center is still a big grass circle where games can be played, and lining the outer or street sides of the circular sidewalk are still small trees and bushes and hedges like those that used to afford us kids great hide-and-seek places.

From the balustrade at the St. Johns River, one could see the modest skyline of the city then (now a grandiose towering skyline) and the Acosta railroad bridge and far across down river over six miles to the other shoreline all the way to the horizon. The dark water was often choppy and a cool breeze could always be counted on but you wouldn't want to swim in it. The weather to me was always the same: warm and nice with frequent, wonderful afternoon rain showers, which I liked to watch from our big front porch.

Modern conveniences
and unintended consequences

Indoor plumbing (as I was to learn later) had only been around since the turn of the century and my grandparent's large two-story, five-bedroom house had been built in 1903, thus had the then modern conveniences of a basin, tub, and flush toilet in each of its two bathrooms upstairs and a basin and toilet in the servants' facility on the back porch. (Before that, there would have been the ubiquitous "out-house" in back yards with its single or double holes in a bench over a dirt pit into which the elimination dropped and which, from time to time, a little powdered lime would be sprinkled over to keep the stench from overpowering, or a covered chamber potty for "night soil" that had to be emptied every morning—one of the first chores of the servants)

From these bathrooms a few snippets of memory remain: In the middle one, I have a distinct recollection of my sitting in the tub in shallow water taking a bath with my mother—Little Buddy—who sat facing me also bathing. I must have been not yet two. And, then I recall her sitting on the toilet and wiping herself from back to front as I watched; I tried that later as I grew and made a mess of it. (Advice to mothers: be careful—your babies can remember more than you might imagine). In the other bathroom, I distinctly recall—at about that same age—my mother standing over me as I stood with my pants dropped down around my ankles at the toilet trying to wee-wee.

It just would not come yet and so my mother kept pouring water from one kitchen pot to another over the toilet bowl until that audible suggestion worked. Upon my proud little achievement, I then announced to her that the pee-pee had been in the little bags under my pee-wee...she persisted gently that no, it came from somewhere else...but I knew she was wrong!

I recall another episode in the end bedroom just off that bathroom: I was about two and Little Buddy was trying to dress me...putting a nice little blue outfit with buttons to a bib strap over the shoulders—but I would have none of it! I remember this distinctly—because there was not a single thought in that empty little head of mine why I did not want to get dressed. I fought and squirmed and resisted and I guess she finally won and we went off somewhere. To this day I recall that there was not a single reason in that little ornery mind of mine at the time for me to have pulled such a tantrum. Child psychologists—"Go figure!"

Another strange performance took place when I was about three: the little three-year-old girl from across the street, Marilyn Medlin, was over to play and we had gotten hold of some peanuts from a dish on a table. For some unfathomable reason known only to the gods, she and I decided to put them on our—or at least mine on my pee-wee and she on her 'whatever'. We then lay on our backs on the side porch, pulled down our panties or diapers or whatever, lifted our legs up and each of us placed a peanut on our thingies—whereupon— to our sheer surprise —Little Buddy appeared quickly out of nowhere and yelled at us. She had us get up, put our pants back on, swatting me on the behind and sending Marilyn home. I gave the whole thing no thought and was back to playing alone in a few minutes oblivious of the previous event.

A frightening event

I remember another time—pretty close to the same age in the above episode and we were at my grandparents'—when late one afternoon my dad came to the front door and banged on it while ringing the doorbell incessantly. Everybody, including the servants rushed to open it—and my dad—all bloody and bruised and muttering—came stumbling in and collapsed on the couch. Mother screamed, the servants ran for towels and water, and my grandparents came quickly.

Dad lay there, his face swollen and the blood dripping down all over his necktie and tweed suit. As mother wiped his face with a cool wet cloth, he slowly explained what had happened—after assuring everyone that nothing was broken:

He had driven his car up north of Jacksonville to the little country dirt crossroads at Callahan to look into a car insurance claim and had stopped at the general store to ask directions. Several grubby white men in dusty overalls (which just about everybody wore back then) who were sitting in front of the store took him for a 'revenuer' man (and, no doubt they had a 'moonshine' still for 'White Lightning' out back) or something like that because he had a car and was dressed in a suit and necktie. So they jumped him—beat him up, clubbed him, really mussed him up...don't know what else...threatened him not to ever come back, or some such, and chased him back into his car which Dad was able and conscious enough to drive the dozen miles or so back to the Averys'.

I remember Daddy Chick lying there for a long time even after he was cleaned up. Don't remember much beyond that terrifying episode so he must have recovered and was not seriously hurt. I later envisioned it like something out of "The Grapes of Wrath"—that is, the country crackers who ruffed him up.

In 1948, the episode was brought back to mind when Dad had a debilitating cerebral hemorrhage that cost him his speech and most mobility by paralysis of his right side. He was then 48 years old and I was a sophomore at Princeton at the time. The doctors had thought the stroke was caused by an earlier blood clot finally reaching a small capillary in the brain. We speculated that this beating a little over decade earlier might have been the cause. Fortunately my father lived another twenty years after the stroke but was unable to take over my Granddaddy Avery's warehouse business as had been planned. The warehouse was ultimately mismanaged by the Florida National Bank and its directors and went bankrupt, was sold, and the family lost its only inheritance.

Friends and neighbors

The neighborhood around my grandparents' house was old and well-established. All the houses and apartment buildings, of course, loomed large to me. Next to my grandparents' on the corner was a vacant lot, upon which later a religious cult erected a small, ugly building that blighted the neighborhood. All the city blocks had sidewalks on all four sides with wide areas of grass between them and the streets. The sidewalks were inlaid with interlocking octagonal cement blocks of slightly different tints. They looked nice but you could not roller skate on them because they were not laid perfectly smoothly, and, the four metal wheels on skates back then were hard enough to make roll anyway (despite oiling) and the cracks and unevenness made it impossible. It was better in the park over by the river.

The side street, May Street, which runs perpendicular to Lomax, was paved in bricks back then so skating on that was totally impossible but the hooves of the mule hauling the ice truck made such a racket on them that it signaled a rally call for all in earshot to run grab some ice chips.

There were a number of playmates in the neighborhood. Marilyn lived across the street, Patty Pilkington on another block, and there were a couple of others whose names I forget. But the most significant was "Sandy." Sandy Brian. He was three years older than I was but was tolerant of my hanging around. He lived with his mother, grandmother, and brother on the first floor of a big brick apartment building right behind my grandparents—allowing for the optician's house that was sort of catty-cornered in between. We all loved the optician; he was kindly and let us kids climb in his small tree in his front yard. Furthermore, he had a fig tree in his side yard and he didn't mind if we helped ourselves and picked a few and ate them while he and his wife watched. Yes, he wore glasses. At the end of May Street lived the big Milam clan with a couple of boys my age, Arthur being the one I recall.

Well, Sandy became my mentor of sorts—he knew everything. I would return home (to the grandparents') for supper and start right off with, "Sandy said...and then keep everybody listening and smiling indulgently right on through the meal to—I hope—their delight. Sandy and I did remain distant friends all our lives although I moved away after college.

One of the things I most benefitted from my friendship with Sandy was his extraordinary ability to build tiny six-inch, balsa-wood and tissue paper models of World War I airplanes. In his dark (all interiors seemed dark to me back then, which is why I tend toward lightness now) bedroom in their apartment, he had a table under the window on which he built them. Onto the little paper plans that came with a kit. he would cut balsa wood strips and stick them over the outlines with straight pins, glueing the pieces together with droplets of banana oil glue, then assembling and glueing them again and covering them with tissue paper and then sprinkling that lightly with water spray to let it dry and tighten, then painting them the accurate colors as they were in the recent war. This is incredible because he could not have been older that seven or eight. (For you moderns who think building model airplanes is simply snapping together plastic forms have no concept of the skill and time required to really build a model airplane the old-fashioned way from the first stick, up. I learned well from Sandy and in my teens built model airplanes from scratch, some of which had 7-foot wingspans and others with accurate details and had workable controls. I strung 100 hundred of them of all sizes from my bedroom ceiling.) When finished, Sandy's were little gems—fragile but perfect in every detail: camouflage, French, English of German identification, guns, and sometimes little figures of the pilots. And, I watched him day in and day out to the point that when I was in First grade I could identify every major World War fighter plane there was. (Keep in mind that in those times everyone looked back on the Great War so recently ended— there was no concept of a Second World War as yet.)

From Sandy, I also learned every major flying "Ace" (5 aerial kills equaled an Ace) on each side of the war as well...including the American Captain Eddie Rickenbacker, our top leading ace who had downed 26 German airplanes. (Incredibly, I was to meet that very American Hero six years later in Atlanta where we were both in the same hospital; Rickenbacker due to a plane crash and me, due to an appendectomy. He autographed and gave me the book he wrote about his WW I flying and I still have it) There is no doubt in my mind that all this led me to an all-consuming interest in aviation as well as delight in later attending the military prep school in Jacksonville, The Bolles School, all during World War II.

Summer Camp, Immokalee

The summer of 1935...when I was seven...some of my shirts and pants, socks, and toothbrush, I guess, were packed up for me in a small suitcase, and Daddy Avery and Big Buddy put that and me in the car and off we went on the road to "Summer Camp," whatever that was. I had no real concept of a 'camp' but was game. They said I would have a lot of fun so I sat contentedly in the big back seat with one hand holding onto the high hand sling that hung from between the widow of the side door and the small triangular one behind it where I could see out.

Finally we arrived in the woods somewhere a long distance from Jacksonville and Lomax Street and everything looked excitingly like a new adventure in store for me. There were no nice houses like back on Lomax; just some wooden sheds in a clearing among the trees. One had a long front porch but no big steps up to the door...it was all flat and everything smelled like trees and air and grass. Well, I had never been in the real woods before so I accepted that this is what it is, after all.

I was led to a small cabin made of rough wood with open windows and met a tall man who was introduced as my Camp Counselor— whatever that meant. His name was "Fletch." Inside were two rows of cots with mattresses and a bunch of other kids who stopped making noise when we entered. Fletch pointed to one of the cots with some folded stuff laying on top and said it was mine. Puzzled, I went over to it and sat on it. Fletch said to tell my folks "Goodbye"...which I did, still somewhat puzzled about what this whole thing was about...but not frightened or trying to cling onto them.

I must have fitted right into the routine because I don't remember much about it. I do recall the lake and how enthralled I was with that compared to the ocean. It didn't have any waves and you could see the bottom. I took to that but stayed in the shallow part. A bunch of older kids were jumping off and splashing around the raft anchored a few yards away. Later Fletch would take us boys from his cabin on walks along the edge of the lake. I would fantasize about floating in the shallow water among the tall plants and big floating leaves (but fortunately didn't—realizing later what possible threats might have lurked there: water moccasins and even alligators!).

I do remember having had a problem those first few days. The bathroom—or 'latrine', as they called it—was a small shed that once you entered the door—and the stink hit you— you were greeted by a long wooden bench on the opposite wall with oval holes holes spaced all the way across it. A couple of kids were sitting on the holes with their pants down around their feet—it was a long potty! I recall approaching and looking down one of the holes where the nasty smells were coming from—and seeing poo-poo and pee pee—I was horrified!—and recoiled and left quickly.

The upshot was that I got real constipated (I don't remember my even peeing) and sort of shied away from the activities. I know I did not go in the lake. Finally after a couple of days Fletch asked me what was wrong...and finally somehow he figured it out and explained that I would have to get used to it and said just not to think about it—and go! He said later that I'd be laughing about pooping there. Once you went, you'd wipe quickly, and turn on the faucet at the wall and the water would wash everything down the tin gutter and it would be flushed— just like at home. I accepted that as fate, I suppose, and got through the full two weeks and still have fond memories and mental images of the place (which probably now has been swallowed up by a retirement community).

Three years later I attended Camp Greenville just over the North Carolina border from the South Carolina city of that name. It, too, was quite rustic but I acclimated quite quickly and well. It was situated in the draw of a small mountain and thus restricted in field activities. The only thing I really remember about that experience was that I contracted the mumps and had to be driven with a couple of other boys and put into the hospital at Greenville—and confined to bed. I couldn't figure why, since I didn't feel all that bad, though my cheeks were bulging like a chipmunk's. We weren't even allowed to get out of bed to pee and poop but had to use a pan while sitting up on the bed. One time as I was sitting on the pan, I was near the window and spotted a car parked within eyesight and a group of negroes in it, so I pulled the sheet up around me a little tighter and heard one of the women shout at me, "Hey, boy, I don't want t' see yo' ass!" That stunned me, because I had never heard anyone use that word—at least in public. Shocking!

In 1943, I attended the larger camp for boys in the low mountains of North Carolina, Camp Carolina. The Jacksonville boys traveled as a group by train that huffed and puffed a stringent cloud of black smoke that got in through all the windows which were kept opened for ventilation—choice: either suffocate with no air or by smoke. We never even thought of air-conditioning, which I guess this old train never had. I had a much better time at this camp where it was fun all the time with much more to do.

One thing I'll never forget, though, was the canoe trip down a nearby river. It was a rainy season and we were advised to take a heavy wool sweater rather than a raincoat; I thought that stupid. Even though wet wool might retain its warmth, you'd still be wet, rather than with a raincoat where you might be cold but you would be dry. Anyway I did take the sweater.

The trip was anything but idyllic. I had expected a cool, clear mountain stream with fish swirling around us and enjoying all the wildlife along the banks. What we encountered was a dark, dank, stinking sewer! It stank just like a sewer—putrid! A fish couldn't have survived anywhere in it. I complained to the counselor about it and he said nothing anyone could do about it...it was all due to the chemicals coming from an industrial plant that dumped its waste into the river. So, that became a first encounter with pollution. It was far from a pleasant outing.

Fun-filled days of summer

Such were the highlights in the Halcyon days in my early youth when I—and later my younger sister—spent the summers with my grandparents. Others back in those uneventful days of the thirties may have found them often boring and dull but not me. Everything was new and exciting. I never was bored nor did I ever ask my parents or grandparents "What is there to do?" I was a doggone little "goody two-shoes"! But, you know? I saw no reason to be bad or disobedient. I never lied to my parents or did devious things or hid anything from them. Everyone around me had good manners so I simply followed their example. Oh...a few times I did something I was not supposed to and I got switched—that is, my mother went into the yard and broke off a long, thin twig and 'switched' it back and forth across my dancing bare legs. It stung like the dickens and I let a tear or two go...and behaved for a long time afterwards.

I do recall a photograph being taken of me sitting in a little cart attached to a billy goat. Evidently an enterprising photographer had this goat cart and would go around neighborhoods and take pictures of children and made a living off that. I was aged four, about the date my sister was born, 1932.

Which do you think was the stubborner?

CHAPTER 6

Other random reflections

My first memorable impressions were from the age of two. I have distinct mental clips of a moment when I was in a stroller all bundled up in cold weather and my mother was pushing it and we were on the sidewalk at the base of a very large viaduct over railroad tracks and buildings. It was not a bright scene...perhaps due to the weather or my memory. It was in Nashville and must have been in 1930.

Another visual snippet was of the apartment we lived in then, and to this day I can still visualize and even draw a picture of it. It was in a big brick building (the Blackstone Apartments) and there was a large side window with many panes of glass in it. (Of course, I could not have known such words back then but was totally aware of my surroundings) Funny that I could remember these two details but not when I strayed away from my nurse and tumbled down some cement basement stairs. Fortunately I was not hurt but my Dad fired the nurse right away, as he told me many years later.

There is a photograph, too, of my mother bundled up in a 1920s-looking coat with a big fur collar and a cloche hat—and little me (still three) in an outfit of leggings that zipped up, an camel overcoat and matching camel cap. We were watching something, probably an air show.

Mother and I in Nashville in 1930. Thirty years later I would dress my own first-born, Avery. Jr., in similar camel coat and cap and take him to New York City to see Disney's "101 Dalmatians"—which he does not remember. I recall it vividly because I had promised him the trip even though I had lost my job as a TV producer in NYC the day before.

This partial memory is intermixed with those of Jacksonville above, since, as I have pointed out, I have no recollection of the traveling in between to get to these other places where we lived.

Rare—but wonderful—treats

Another vivid memory and a very delicious one was ice cream. Occasionally, of course, we kids were treated to an ice cream cone—the waffle type, twisted into a cone with that always dripping tiny hole in the bottom and a scoop of the goodie on top for us to lick, finally bite into, and devour with the cone. Nothing better?

Well, how about churned "home-made" ice cream? Daddy Avery had one of those small wooden bucket types with a contraption across the top that held something that turned when you cranked the attached handle. Rock salt, I believe it was—was then mixed with ice in the area around a central core that held the cream and vanilla (I don't ever remember chocolate), and when the handle was cranked and cranked for a long time it would freeze the contents inside the center core into wonderful home-made ice cream. That was really a treat. That, along with sitting on the edge of the back porch with a big juicy red slice of watermelon and biting, spitting the seeds out onto the ground, and finally slurping the sweet stuff right down to the white of the rind.

Toys, back in the 1930s, were well made, sturdy, some kind of metallic material—way before plastics were invented. There were some very cheap small toys of boats and airplanes made of wood but they were crummy, didn't look accurate and had "Made in USA" stamped on the back. Even then at a tender age we knew that that meant they were made in Japan; somebody had pointed out that the Japanese were great copiers and that they had a city in Japan named "USA" where they manufactured all this cheap stuff and sold it to the Americans (maybe swapped for our scrap iron and steel?—as we were later also aware of) The toy section of a department store was tucked way in the back and only consisted of a couple of counters. Some of the most enticing were large toy trucks...dump trucks whose rear part would pivot so you could put some dirt in it and actually dump it! But toys were only for special occasions—not for every time we visited a store.

That made us all the more anxious—and anticipating getting one for a birthday or Christmas, which were the only occasions we could expect presents, anyway. I remember one time my mother did buy me a small "Fireman's hat." All kids loved firemen, policemen, soldiers, cowboys, etc, and "play-acted" them all the time, although I never had any desire to grow up to be a fireman or a policeman. The hat was (now that I am thinking about it) a light gauzy orange material molded in the shape of the Fireman's. A whole stack of them were just waiting to be bought. Mother would not let me wear it home. But, when Dad came home from work, he took it out in the yard and poured some gasoline over it. This, he said, was to sterilize it from germs picked up in the stores (parents were ever fearful back then of children picking up something horrible like polio from public places). Well, even after Dad let the gasoline dry off it still stank so I never wore it.

Another time, when we were living in Columbia, South Carolina, in the early '30s, a grocery store had a stack of imitation World War "tin-pot" helmets—junior sized. And, they were red. I wanted one badly but Little Buddy would not buy it for me and I pouted the rest of the day. Earlier, when we were living in Atlanta (the first time), I had seen a comic book or a movie about the jungle explorer Frank Buck—and I wanted to be a "Frank Buck" explorer so bad I pestered about it all the time. When my Dad had to go out of town on a brief trip, I begged him to bring me back a "Frank Buck" suit. I couldn't sleep awaiting that; I wanted to go up to nearby Ponce de Leon Avenue and explore behind some bushes in back of a row of stores there—in my Frank Buck (pith) helmet, shorts, and (safari) jacket. When Dad returned without it—I was unconsolable! I pulled tantrum after tantrum—all to no avail. I think they just ignored me after patiently explaining that there were none for sale—anywhere! Such are the painful disillusions of childhood.

The first, short move to Atlanta...

...Which brings to mind that first time we lived in Atlanta in 1932-33: We lived in an upstairs apartment in NE a couple of blocks off Peachtree and north of Ponce de Leon (probably around Penn and 5th).

61

Margaret Mitchell's home was also nearby but nobody had heard of her back then. On our second move to Atlanta in 1939-40, she, of course, was world famous not only from her monumental book—that erroneously portrayed nasty lo' Sherman's burning of Atlanta toward the end of the War Between the States (aka The Civil War) but from the movie of "Gone With the Wind" that debuted there in 1939 at the Fox Theater with all the attendant Hollywood folderol.

Anyway, at the top of the stairs, to the right, was the bathroom; a few steps past it were the two bedrooms and to the left of the stairs was the living room and off that, a glassed-in porch. My sister was a little past one year old and I was a little past four and I remember our being allowed to run freely upstairs stark naked before getting into the bath tub to be given our baths together. Other than that, I only recall the Frank Buck episode and snow. One day we looked out and snow covered the ground (I had remembered seeing it in Nashville) but this was not good snow to play in. It was hard, ice-crusted on top and too deep for my short little legs to navigate.

Then to: Columbia, South Carolina

Evidently my father was succeeding in his insurance claims business or we probably would not have moved so often. He might have been a trouble-shooter of some sort.

My next recollections are from a charming little bungalow in Columbia up on a hill from Five Points and around on Myrtle Court, a tiny cul-de-sac. I say, charming little bungalow, because in retrospect it was very reminiscent, not only of the architecture of the 1920s, but looked just like the quaint houses in Walt Disney's movie cartoons: the little steeped roof that came down to frame the front door, the brick veneer, and the mullioned windows. (I have always had a pretty good knack for directions and 'spatial relations' and upon researching Myrtle Court on Google Earth, I'm darned if I don't think what is now labelled Rice Court [now either *in* or *next* to Wales Garden] was the original Myrtle Court, which is now listed as a short dead-end street below Rice. I hope Google is wrong. I know the original Myrtle Court paralleled

Saluda Avenue, and the area south now bordered by Barnwell Street down to Wheat was all the negro section about which I write. The railroad tracks below Wheat and adjacent to where Saluda bends up from Five Points were where we surreptitiously adventured).

Good old A.C. More Elementary is still where it has always been, there on S. Wacamaw Ave and Rosewood. The other primary school I attended, I guess, for the second half of the first grade when we moved was somewhere over to the north around something like 'Shandon."

Disney's "Snow White and the Seven Dwarfs" had come out in 1934 and I can't quite remember whether I saw it in Columbia or Tampa, our next move. It was so marvelously engaging that I still have vivid mental pictures of every frame of it. Anyway, back before in Jacksonville, I do remember previously seeing the first Mickey Mouse cartoons, "Steamboat Willie," and the "Three Little Pigs," all now historical classics. "Snow White," though, was breath-taking. I could not stop dreaming about it and there were books and articles and pictures and that was one of the most talked about things of the times—a great morale booster for the Depression. It took everyone's minds off their miseries for a while.

In Columbia, though, the comparable fantasy was the movie "Babes in Toy Land," a Victor Herbert musical, as I researched but do not recall—or they meant nothing to me at the time—that the comedians Laurel and Hardy starred in it. The "March of the Toy Soldiers" had us marching all around the house and the neighborhood with folded paper hats and toy drums to the music still swirling in our heads.

Part of what I remember in vivid flash-back is incredible—and would be child abuse today: I think it was the summer before I turned six—I know it was prior to my entering the first grade in Columbia. There I was, still in a baby suit, that is, my pants held up by two big buttons attached to my shirt (just like Mickey Mouse?). And, down at the end of Myrtle Court were two of my same-aged playmates: "Pap" and "Lamek." Well, together we were quite adventurous, if not a bit innocently devious.

Leading out of the paved cul-de-sac in front of their house was a foot path in the dirt through a break in the shrubbery that opened onto a dirt road in the negro section of town (now Barnwell St.?). To the left,

63

the road led past some shacks to a general store at the corner of another dirt road. Back the other way, the dirt road led down to the railroad tracks below where Wheat Street ended—all this behind the cultivated white neighborhood built off Saluda Avenue and where we lived. Many is the time we—*imagine!—at age five!*—would go walk along the railroad tracks in curiosity...often led by the attendant stench to the dried carcasses of cats or other small animals that had been run over by the trains. Often we encountered a "hobo"; we seemed to know that term back then: a poor guy out of work "riding the rails" with others in empty boxcars from one city to another looking for work or a lot of times camping for days or months under bridge trestles sharing whatever they had with other hobos. Most evidently were docile— harmless—but you never could have even thought that one might get drunk on some ill-gotten moonshine and cause a ruckus—or hurt somebody—*or attack us!* The railroad "Dicks" (Dick Tracys) were alway shooing them away.

Sometimes, we'd spot a flattened penny next to the tracks where someone had put it to see what the train running over it would do to it. So, we, too, would do the same thing—whenever we found a stray penny to do it with. After all, a penny was worth something back then, as was a nickel. There was something called a "Wooden Nickel." I think that had something to do with the Depression. I thought, of course, it would be round like the real one but was puzzled to get hold of one and it turned out to be a thin wooden rectangle with blue words on it. (I have since found out it was, indeed, a sort of promotion by banks and the Chamber of Commerce during the Depression. Later, other wooden nickels were produced as promotional schemes in assorted round shapes and sizes.)

Actually, if we did have a penny or two, we'd rather walk up the other way on the dirt road to the general store in the black neighborhood. We thought nothing of it since our nurses and cooks were all blacks and friendly. So, toddling along in our little-boy garb and dusty sandals, we'd reach up and open the tattered screen door and walk into the musty interior...and up to the counter where the old black man in worn overalls took the money. The other black people would look on, some in amusement, as some probably knew us from working for the "white folks" in our neighborhood; none, though, ever told our parents, thinking they must have known. Anyway, we knew exactly what we wanted: a penny strawberry candy stick.

Once we had made our purchase and unwrapped it, we would slowly walk back sucking on the candy stick until it was gone before we reached the hole in the hedge and wandered home. Neither of these escapades did we ever think important enough to tell our parents—nor did my mother ever ask me where we had been. God knows what she would have done had she known! Back in those days, however, there was not the incipient danger that there is today in a tiny white kid wandering about a black neighborhood.

One very disturbing thing I remember and still cannot believe it was commonly done back then. When my mother took me to a shoe store to buy and new pair, I tried them on and the floor salesman ushered me and my mother over to a tall wooden device. He told me to stick my feet into the slot at the bottom then he turned on a light and looked down a scope of some sort. He then told my mother to do so and explained how well the fit was. I then got the chance to look into the scope and was startled to see my bones! My foot bones! All whitish against a blueish background. The salesman proudly announced that we were looking straight through a 'living' X-Ray! (It was a fluoroscope). It was incredible and I wanted to linger and watch the bones in my feet move when I wiggled them. Fortunately, we did not linger and left with the new pair of, I think, boots...it was snowy at the time. But—good grief—what they did not know about radiation back then. I wonder how many unsuspecting people accumulated too many roentgens of radiation from that simple attraction—and later developed cancer?

Although my Dad must have driven me to A.C. Moore each morning, I do have vague recollections of walking home. Could that have been? There was very little automobile traffic in those days and I do recall a lot of kids walking with me, but that was quite a distance down S. Waccamaw over to Saluda, then down Myrtle Court. I know that when we moved to the other house way over on the other side of Saluda Avenue, the school was only a couple of blocks away and I did walk to and from. I don't remember the name of that school but it was somewhere near Blossom or Devine, again up from Five Points and is now a condominium. I must have completed the second half of the first grade there, because I remember entering the second grade in Tampa.

Time back then passed so much slower than it does later in life and that gave all of us young kids more time for school and play and memories. Would that were so today.

On Myrtle Court in Columbia, South Carolina, 1934

CHAPTER 7

Now in Tampa

Our rented house at 2418 Watrous Avenue in Tampa where we lived from about 1934 through 1936.

While the periods of living in Atlanta and Columbia were pleasant —and Jacksonville was the redeeming core—Tampa was really the foundational habitat.

There we lived in two different houses and I advanced from second through sixth grades.

I adored school and couldn't wait every day to be off. Usually, after I got myself dressed, either she or the cook would make me a sandwich and put an orange or something with it in a paper bag for my lunch, and my Dad would drop my sister and me off on his way to work. From the fifth grade I think I walked home after school...dawdling with friends along the way ending up at home—about two miles away—in late afternoon. Mother only worried about me one time, as I recall, due to my probably overstaying my visit in the yard of a little girl who I assume attracted me. Mother seemed upset but I could not figure out why.

Yours truly, Daddy Chick, and sister Catherine, c. 1935. He used to tell us that if we crawled under bushes and houses we would get "creeping corruption," and if we ate something that did not agree with us, we would get the "collywobbles."

Across the street from us lived one of my best friends, Billy Armstead. In the backyard of their one-story house was a wonderful tree next to the house and the lower limbs were right within reach. The upper ones were easy to climb up to and were at about roof-top level. Those branches just beckoned climbing—where most of us kids in the neighborhood could always be found at 'round-up' time for supper. Of course, we were filled with the exploits of Tarzan in the Saturday afternoon serials at the movies—swinging from tree-top to tree-top with all the ease of a trapeze artist, so we aped the marvelous things he did swinging from tree to tree—except that we, of course, were not as adept as either Tarzan, the "King of the Jungle," or his simian sidekick, "Cheeta"—so it was bound to happen: "Me—*Tarzan*" no make it to other branch—and "Me no Cheeta" either—flopped right down squarely on my back (fortunately it was only from about five feet up). I hollered like a stuck pig and Mrs. Armstead and the cook came running out to see if I bad broken anything; fortunately I was whole, maybe bruised a bit, but determined never ever try to out-Tarzan *Tarzan* again. Furthermore, as much as we all tried, not a one of us could ever come close to duplicating the loud, yodeling call that Tarzan made as he swung through the tree-tops; only comedienne Carol Burnett was able to do so decades later, a thing that became her trademark of sorts—and she was called on to render it in most of her public appearances. (The film version was probably an artificial audio track creation)

No, nothing was broken that time but a bit later—and I remember this vividly: I was seven—were were all playing at Billy's and there was a wooden fence from his garage lining the property line all the way to the sidewalk. The supporting structure naturally was on the inside—the long 2x4s along the bottom and just under the top where the pointed pickets were. Well, I guess it was Tarzan again—or maybe "Boy" this time—but I decided to try to creep along this upper inside board while holding on to the pickets for balance. My being bent over with my rump up like a camel was too much temptation for Billy—he gave me— *it*!—a shove with a long stick he was carrying—and over I went onto the neighbor's driveway...and crashed onto it on my left elbow. Billy, of course, laughed and high-tailed it into his house. I, on the other hand— or arm, I should say—rolled over bawling like all get-out and ran across the street to Mother, holding my injured arm that was hurting like the dickens.

She immediately tried to calm me and survey the damage while I jumped around holding it and wailing. It was obvious to her that it was broken and the rest is slightly dimmed in memory. I know we went to a doctor—I don't know that there were any Emergency Rooms at the hospitals back then. I suppose there were but I do remember being in a doctor's office and his taking my left arm gingerly—probably re-setting the break—and then—my Gosh!—he crooked it up—meaning bent the broken elbow up against my chest with my left hand just under my chin —and as either Mother or a nurse held it—and me—the doctor took a big wide role of adhesive tape—much wider than what you put on a cut —and began to wrap my poor broken elbow-arm to my chest...round and round...all the way around my back and again over the now immobile arm. If I had known what a straight-jacket was at the time, I would have equated it with that. I was totally strapped! Couldn't move that left arm, of course, and found it a bit hard to breathe. Fortunately, I did not envision the consequences of when all that adhesive tape would be coming off. I looked like a half-mummy.

The upshot of all this was that I would have to stay this way for about six weeks...keep the tape dry...don't recall how I bathed or whether Mother or the maid bathed me—certainly not in the tub (There were no showers with tubs back then, or at least we never had one). So, the weeks went by and I went to school and had much explaining to do and was the source of a lot of attention...getting out of recess and having to sit and watch the others.

Then came the reckoning! I had not really dwelled on or thought seriously about the consequences. Mother had assured me that taking off the adhesive tape would be nothing to worry about—the doctor would squirt some ether (there's that awful thing again!)—and it wouldn't hurt at all. So, she convinced me. But, believe me, I still remember it. It was an ordeal...the first layers, of course, came off quite easily since they were stuck onto underlying layers of tape; it was when he got down to bare skin that trouble began. Ether be danged! The doctor had to squirt and peel just a tiny bit at a time—and the fumes of the ether had me terrified by a not-long-ago memory of the tonsils. After a long, long time in my time-clock; it was all off, exposing my raw, whitish tender skin. The Doc then gently eased my arm down and slowly flexed the elbow. It didn't hurt but was stiff and I could not bend it all the way. Due to that, I had another six weeks of discomfort: every time I had to walk anywhere I had to carry in that left hand a little tin toy bucket like you play with in a sandbox or at the beach—filled up with sand as a weight to keep pulling that elbow back down to its normal position. That was a real drag! (Of course, we didn't use that term back then.) I probably pleaded, "Do I haffta? Really?"

I'm here to tell you, it was a real chore but it worked and the arm healed perfectly, thank goodness.

While I'm on ailments, about this same time but at Easter, we all, of course, dressed up in our finest: Dad in a new light colored suit—and me in a grey little-man's imitation and a man's type gray straw hat (I cringe when I see the photo!). My sister in her little pinafore dress and bonnet...Mother all dolled up with gloves and a little hat with a veil over the face—as she always dressed up to go to church.

Well, during all that something came over me and I started to have chills—or at least I asked Mother for my coat because I told her I was cold—and it was a terribly hot day. So, she felt my forehead and, yes, I had a fever. So, when we got home—to bed I went and the liquids started. Any sickness —for any parent—is frightening—and more so back then with so little to overcome illnesses, much less dreading what it might lead to. (Having been through this sort of thing with my own children, I can't begin to imagine the terror that must have been struck in the hearts of mothers back then, especially my Mother, since her teenaged brother had died from tetanus from a simple basketball injury.)

Aside from the mustard plaster or Vicks Vapor Rub applied to the chest for colds and coughs—and sensibly plenty of liquids —there was one   home remedy that I can

71

still taste, it was so awful! In a teaspoon of sugar, my Mother put a few drops of turpentine—yes, *turpentine*—over the sugar and gave it to me to swallow. I did—gagged—just about threw up—and, as I write, I can still taste that horrible thing to this very day. Dreadful. Much worse than castor oil.

Flashbacks of the 1930s

As most kids did back then in the fourth grade, I joined the Cub Scouts. Once I got that uniform, I think I wore it even to bed! I know there were certain days when Cub Scout meeting followed after school, I proudly wore it to school as did other boys. And, I usually wore it on Saturday afternoon trips that we took in the family car, too.

At one time—or maybe all the time—whatever, I never paid any attention to it, I just fitted into whatever the routine of life was...but we must have had two cars. I know that my Dad had to travel and that my mother, sister, and I were bound to have been driven places and the maid home once in a while. And, because I remember vividly one time late one Friday afternoon when Dad drove into the driveway after a long trip down in South Florida. Even on those primitive two-lane country roads he said he streaked along at sometimes 80 miles an hour. His car was a blue coupe—

*cou-**pé***—as it was pronounced back then. It was a two-seater—I don't recall any back seat—and I know it was not a "roadster" with a rumble seat that popped up out of the hump on the back that was also used to store baggage. There had been cars with canvas tops that could be lowered in older cars in the 1920s but I don't recall any in the '30s; there was no such thing as a 'convertible'—at least I never heard that term.

Anyway, coming home from a long trip, Dad drove into our driveway and we all went out to greet him. As he opened his door and started to get out, the steering wheel came right off in his hands! He just stood there paralyzed...holding the steering wheel up to look at it to make sure he was seeing right, then turned to us with a startled look on his face...that was echoed in ours—all thinking at the same time what a close call! If that wheel had come off when he was doing 80 down a country road—or any road—!!!

Cars were just cars back then. Nothing very fancy, at least not to the ordinary family. The "Chords," "Packards," big "Pierce Arrows" were only rarely seen, if at all. Most cars were simply functional, no frills, you had to hand crank down the windows—which were down most of the time since air-conditioning was not even dreamed of then—cooling the car when driving was called "2-60," two windows down at 60 miles an hour! There were usually two little triangular window vents on each side of the front windshield, which was two plates of glass with a metal strip in the middle holding them together. The windshield wipers—if there were two—flap-flapped back in forth in counter sync. If the driver wanted to signal a turn, he/she had to roll down his window and stick his/her left hand out: straight, if the turn was to the left; lower arm straight up for a right turn. In rain the arm got wet. Of course, seat belts were not yet dreamed of so there was a hanging strap on each side of the back seat but nothing for the front seat passenger to hold onto or grab. And, that front seat spanned the width of the car: both the front and back seats were simply padded benches. If a third person sat in the middle up front, he/she could expect to straddle between his/her knees the long gear shift rod and handle that came up from the floor board. A more expensive car would have perhaps a fold-down arm rest in the middle. With sudden stops everyone got tussled up a bit trying to hold onto something.

Traveling long distances was done but with some trepidation. There was no connecting highway system and no rest stops, much less predictable gasoline "filling" stations along the way. All the roads were two-lanes, hard-topped but with lots of pot holes and uneven concrete, cracks and such. Another thing, at least in the South, or whenever we drove somewhere in Florida or Georgia going up to Atlanta, there was another danger: cows on the roads. Back then there were no so-called "Fencing-in" laws requiring farmers and cattle ranchers (and Florida was and still is a big cattle producing state) to fence in their herds so let them graze anywhere...paid no mind if they crossed a road for greener pastures or not—"t'wern't none a' them city folks'es business, no how!" So, we'd be cruising along usually about 60 miles and hour or so and suddenly around a bend—Screech!—a bunch of cows moseying along on the sides and crossing the highway. At night, it was particularly dangerous—and scary. The headlights of the cars were not what they are today so you would come up on the dark figures of the beasts again quite suddenly and have to slam on the breaks. Sometimes, somebody would have to get out of the car and shoo them off before proceeding.

It was bad enough traveling by car with children who when least expected cried out, "I gotta go pee pee!" For them, it was stop by the side of the road, but for the grownups it was a little more difficult. Especially with a negro servant along as well, it really presented a problem. As if the facilities at Filling stations were not worse than some even today, back then there was absolute segregation, which meant no facilities at all for "Coloreds." I remember we always somehow stopped and the adults—including the servant—got out and managed to bid Nature's callings. That was repeated whenever we had to stop for lunch or to get gas or a bottle of Coca Cola. Most of the time a lunch bag was prepared for the servant while the white folks entered the diner to eat. Gasoline stations were few and far between and, of course, they didn't stay open very late, especially in the country were in some places electricity had just reached them and were not left on for very long. Gasoline was a little over a dime a gallon and the pumps had big round glass bulbs on top with names like Esso, Texaco, Ethyl, Shell, Sinclair, etc. As today, all cars also had either one or two spare tires either on the back trunk or on on each side positioned in a cutout part of the rear of each front bumper. You didn't make a long trip in those days without having to resort to using one or two—and to replace it yourself! I remember some of the fire trucks had what looked like just thick rubber tires. All vehicles were stick shifts—no modern automatic drive. I remember advertisements back around 1940 when Chrysler introduced "Fluid Drive," which captured the fancy of the public but must not have been able to be delivered until after the coming war.

Our trusty car around 1938. Most cars all looked alike to me.

Fun and games

There were no organized team sports for kids back then, not even the Cub Scouts or Boy Scouts had any since both organizations emphasized individual achievement over the group. Therefore, any softball, touch football, or whatever were typical "pick-up" games that spontaneously sprang up on vacant lots or school grounds after hours. I don't even remember many high school teams but I suppose there were some; we didn't have any in elementary school (1st through 6th grades).

There were lots of vacant lots in Tampa around where we lived on Watrous and Jetton Avenues, bounded by Morrison and Howard just a mile or so from Tampa Bay. It never occurred to me but I imagine the housing developments—such as they were during the Depression—were mostly on hold. I certainly don't recall there being but one or two new houses ever being built back then. So, with all those vacant lots scattered around neighborhoods like ours that had been built in the 1920s, there was ample room to play everywhere. Between our house on Watrous and the next one to our left was a small vacant lot that the previous owners of ours and the opposite owner's properties had bought for protection and had kept it grassed and we shared its mowing. It was a great place to romp, 'wrassle', play crack-the-whip (where one kid stays in place and others join arms in a line, then they start spinning in a circle, faster and faster, until the kid on the end can't hold on any longer and is spun off, tumbling head over heels to everyone's glee), or just roll over and enjoy the soft verdant grass (and I never did get a flea), and, of course, throw baseballs and footballs. The little girls had their own hopscotch games going on the sidewalk, throwing a stone or something onto one of the chalked blocks they had drawn in the shape of repeating single and double squares, then hopping on one leg onto each square to reach the 'object' thrown successively into one of the squares, bending over and picking it up— still keeping the other foot raised—turning and then hopping back on that one leg to the starting point. We boys would take over once in a while and mock the girls by doing it faster and rougher. Our ground game was, instead, marbles. And everyone carried some in his pockets, or at least his favorite agate. The neighbors were tolerant of our hijinks and just let us work it off. As evening bore on, we kids would be allowed to stay until the lightening bugs came out so we could chase them and clap them into mason jars with a cloth that we punched air holes in so they could breathe. They were all dead by morning, of course. Oh, what happy times, those.

Right behind Billy Armstead's house across the street were two or three vacant lots together, a bit overgrown but good enough to stomp out a baseball diamond. And, we played hardball, we pre-teens. I had a first-baseman's glove that I broke in real well, mostly by my Dad throwing really hard stuff at me. So, that was fun playing and getting all hot and dirty.

There was one mishap that stymies me to this day: Billy's Dad had been pitching to us for batting practice and Billy had gone into his house for a minute.

So, his Dad pitched to me. After missing a few, I struck one right on!—a hard, straight drive—right into the right eye socket of Mister Armstead!

He lurched back, stunned momentarily, then grasped his face with his two hands—didn't utter a sound—and stumbled through the back gate and into his house. I scooted home as fast as I could. I didn't know what to do. I told my Mother and then I disappeared in my room and closed the door. I hope, to this day, that she called Mrs. Armstead—or Dad, did Mister—and apologized for me or offered to pay for any medical help. My memory is a total blank as to what transpired afterward. I think Billy and I didn't play together for a while...and I don't think we ever talked about the incident. I hope Mr. Armstead didn't end up like my Dad with a hemorrhage like he did from that earlier beating that I wrote about previously.

We kids on our blocks didn't mess with the kids two blocks down; they didn't appear very friendly. We stayed away from them and they, us. Our gang did a lot of improvisation. There were a lot of palm trees around and their big spreading dead leaves and long stems would be cut down or blown down by the wind—or just dry up and drop off. Anyway, we made all sorts of things out of them, carving such things as swords with our pocket knives. Every kid had a pocket knife with him at all times; sometimes we even wore larger fishing or camping knives in their sheaths on our belts. Grownups never worried about us or told us not to carry them. The same with BB guns, of which every kid had one and carried it around and played and shot things with it all the time. Once, in the fourth or fifth grade, the teacher gave us an assignment to draw a bird. I drew a Meadow Lark that looked quite good. When the teacher asked me about it, I admitted that I had gone into a field near our house and shot it with my BB gun. *Horrors*—upon *Horrors*! The teacher scolded me in front of the class and made me go sit in the cloak room for the rest of the period. I don't know why she got so ruffled...all of us kids would go out and shoot stuff, tin cans...trees...flowers...birds. So what? (Well, I realized many years later, the poor little mother Meadowlark was just trying to protect her nest and was leading me away from it when I—*the great Frank Buck*—did her in.)

I never told her that we also picked up the weed 'rabbit tobacco' growing in a field and tried to smoke it—but never succeeded. We'd put a short stalk between our lips and light the other end—and it just flamed out. Otherwise, we were not devilish and did not do destructive or bad things. We were pretty good, overall...no fights...no trouble, either in the neighborhood or in school. We just lived a very pleasant childhood in much calmer days with far fewer distractions and trivia. We would ride our junior-sized bicycles up to the drug store and flop them down on the sidewalk and go inside and read as many comic books as we could get away with before being hustled to move on.

The comic strips and early evening radio were the entertainment of the times, interspersed with a Saturday movie matinee always with a recurring shorter, 'Cliff-Hanging' serial of "Tom Mix," "Red Ryder," "Hop-a-Long Cassidy," or the "Lone Ranger." Later they all became radio serials that just before supper every day were a must—homework or not! Great for being out of the way while supper was being prepared and Dad was coming home from work. Of course, those of us who wanted to be cowboys when we grew up would wear a red bandana just like Hoppy's around our necks when we were playing and even to school. We always managed to get a little cowboy hat and every kid had a two-gun holster for his two cap pistols as well. Of course, our make-believe would not have been complete without that Red Ryder BB gun. We also had land sleds—"Flexi-Flyers." They were varnished wood strips set on two small back wheels and the front wheels were on a steering handle flush with the main frame and just six inches off the ground. You grabbed the handles and ran along then plopped yourself down onto it like on a sled—except you were on the sidewalk instead of snow. Every boy had one and we propelled ourselves or another pushed you all around the neighborhood. They and bicycles were our trusty steeds.

A Cuban connection & 'Injuns'

Across the street and down a house or two a Cuban family moved in with a bunch of kids younger than we were, so we didn't play with them —and they didn't speak English anyway. The father went off to work each day—probably in "EE-bor" ("Ybor") City on the other side of Tampa where most Cuban immigrants lived and most worked in the cigar factories or restaurants there. The mother was big and fat and we hadn't seen many people like that back then. She didn't speak any English either but was loud and always calling after her kids playing in the yard: "Benaka-Cheeko!" (which I found out much later when I studied Spanish was actually: "Ven acá, chico!" which meant, "Come here, boy!")

Dad would drive us over just past downtown Tampa to the northeast to Ybor City once in a while and it was like another world, sort of. It was the "Latin Quarter" back then but I had no idea what that was. Cuba then was a friendly neighbor and a favorite tourist destination, although none of us ever went there. The Ybor streets were wide, there were a few buildings, and the line of stores and restaurants contained a number of little cigar stores. An *hombre* would be seated behind the front window at a table for passers-by to watch him make the cigars. He would grab a tobacco leaf, roll it expertly into its final, recognizable shape, then lick the final end with his tongue to seal the wrapping before slipping a snug ring label down it to hold it fast—then stacking it with the others he had finished.

Another thing we would do would be to play "Indians" with costume feathered headdresses, bare chests and dish rag over our belts as a loin cloth. Down at the beach house one time, a friend and I decided to make 'real' loin cloths. So, we took off our pants and underpants and folded long dishtowels from the kitchen...brought them up under our crotch at the front and the back and under our belts, letting the flaps fall both covering our fronts and the back sides. We went around the house whooping and hollering and stomping up and down as if in a Warrior War Dance—much to the amusement of Big Buddy who tolerated our innocence.

I was enthralled by Indian lore. There were wonderful pictures (illustrations) in our second and third-grade school books that showed Indians in great forests, clad only in loin cloths, a couple of feathers in their hair, and moccasins on their feet creeping silently through the woods. I wanted to do that so bad, I had to try to construct something similar. So, after suffering interminable begging from me, my parents bought me a canvas Teepee that I went right about setting up in the lush grass in the back yard. It became stifling hot inside after a while but—we *Braves*—could bear it. It was a thrill squatting in it during a cloud burst—except that water ran in under the staked bottom of the tent and ruined our fantasy and soaked our pants.

Years later, one of my sons interested in genealogy discovered a very intricate 19th Century circular chart of all of the Chenoweth ancestry. One particular line could be traced back through the Randolph and Rolf lines directly to John Rolf who married the Indian Chief's daughter, Pocahontas, who had saved John Smith from execution at the Jamestown, Virginia, settlement in 1609. Rolf and his new wife Pocahontas moved to England where their son, James Rolf, was born. After "Lady" Pocahontas died prematurely, father and son moved back to Virginia to farm. Son James' line is the generation that ultimately mingled with the Chenoweths. If this, indeed, be true, I am especially proud to think I might have the blood of Pocahontas' father, The Great Chief Powhatan, coursing in my clogging veins.

In the spirit of full disclosure: an off-shoot of the Chenoweths evidently migrated to Liberia, Africa—that is, some of the slaves the pioneering Chenoweths had in Maryland in the early 18th Century. If you remember, our fourth president, James Monroe—or some members of Congress at the time—formulated a plan in the early 19th Century to send all the slaves in America back to Africa. The intended location was what is now Liberia, and to that effect, the Capital there is named Monroeville, in honor of that president. Evidently, some Chenoweth slaves did migrate—and took the name there with them. I discovered this only recently here in Georgia when a black woman saw my name and said she had relatives by that name in Liberia. I surmised the rest of the story. My step-son-in law was once stationed in the U.S. State Department there (*before Ebola*) and I asked him to look them up, but he was not successful.

A fantastic Safari

There was a streetcar line a few blocks away. It must have been down Howard Street then paralleled down the railroad tracks that ran all the way down beyond the built-up area of the city to the end of the peninsula that jutted into Tampa Bay. (It would have been under the present Selmon Expressway) That was a pretty barren area in the mid '30s, not densely populated like it became later, especially when the U.S. Army Air Corps Base, McDill Field was built there just before World War Two. The fare for a round trip was fifteen cents and the trip took a couple of hours. So, all week we'd scrape up 25 cents by chores or allowance to take the trolley trip on Saturday. The extra dime was to treat ourselves afterwards to an ice cream soda at the drug store on the corner of Howard and Watrous just past the angular railroad crossing. We'd often have to stop with our bicycles there when a long train came through. Often we'd see open freight cars loaded with scrap iron and even then we had heard that this was all being shipped to Japan. Little did we ever think it would be coming back at us a few years later in the form of bullets and bombs.

The slow and jiggly ride on the trolley tracks never bothered us, our make-believe world was full of imagined descriptions of visions of herds of buffalos, or giraffes, or charging lions...elephants...saying you were sure you spotted Tarzan...or Chief Sitting Bull...or Hopalong Cassidy riding through the bush—which is what we had to describe the prevalent palmettos. At the end, the conductor would pause for ten minutes or so before going to the opposite end of the car to operate the controls to run backwards on the return trip. He just flopped the wicker cane seats over then to sit facing forward. I don't remember our taking a canteen of water along although we might have because I remember I had somehow collected various Boy Scout paraphernalia. The heat never bothered us; probably we did not even get thirsty. The anticipated soda would take care of that, anyway.

When McDill got going under construction, and the runways operational, Army airplanes would often fly overhead. It would eventually become during its early phase a training base for the new, four-engined B-17 "Flying Fortress" bombers. Sometime during all this, either at McDill or over at the municipal airport just west of the city, there were displays of military prototype (a word I never heard) aircraft and I could identify and name most of them (thank you, Sandy Brian).

The early model Boeing B-17 Flying Fortress with the early U.S. insignia with the red dot in the star as they looked flying from McDill Field over Tampa

Other excitements

"Gasparilla" was an anticipated annual event that captured the imagination of the entire city and news of it spread far and wide. It was a community-wide celebration harking back to supposed times when "Pirates" sailed in and out of Tampa in the early part of the 18th Century under their captain, José Gaspar. A real three-masted sailing ship accompanied by a flotilla of private small boats would come up Tampa Bay and up the Hillsborough River with sails billowing, whistles blowing, horns blaring, and cannon booming, and crowds along the waterfronts cheering and screaming and bands playing...and a good time being had by all. That was followed by the costumed pirates (played by members of a social club, "Ye Mystic Krewe of Gasparilla" and under the auspices of the city) who then took over the city in a big parade downtown, somewhat like a 'Mardi Gras.'

I remember watching the parade from my Dad's office window on the second floor. Back then the was no air-conditioning so office windows opened and there were no screens—one could easily fall out—or pigeons fly in—not to mention mosquitoes. I was firmly held as I watched all the commotion not really grasping what it was all about other than a lot of color, noise, and seeming fun.

The young Buccaneer himself

Another public event was amusing and did not ruin my appreciation of the Santa Claus myth—I was old enough not to believe in him but my sister still did. It was a bit startling, though, to have Santa Claus arrive in Tampa at the appointed time after Thanksgiving (which had just been re-proclaimed by President Roosevelt as the third Thursday each November)—in a yellow Piper Cub seaplane setting down on the water of the Hillsborough River.

Yep. In came the little plane and smoothly setting itself down on its two pontoons right in the middle of the river in front of the cheering crowds on each bank...and then a portly Santa clumsily struggled out with his big bag (filled with balloons I suppose since the little Piper could not carry much weight, as I knew from my ride in one) trying to step gingerly onto the pontoon and being helped onto the dock. What an image! Only a Hawaiian Santa in a Hula skirt would have been more disillusioning—except, I understand that in Honolulu, Hawaii, Santa does arrive now on water skies!

One thing that was far from disillusioning was baseball. Tampa had the good fortune to be the winter training location for the Cincinnati Reds. Consequently, demonstration training games with other teams wintering in Florida became a main attraction and a more pleasant way to spend a Saturday afternoon was not to be found. Dad took me and my friends to many a game. We went to one in Punta Gorda down the West Coast of the Gulf of Mexico. I was in my Cub Scout uniform so I must have been around seven or eight (1936?) and there was some mention of Babe Ruth (he retired in 1934)—but I have no recollection of whether I really saw him or not—nor Lou Gehrig—in any of those exhibition games.

I probably saw other famous athletes, people, and aviators, but only remember tennis player Don Budge's name in particular (and taught myself basic tennis from his instructional book many years later).

Up several blocks from Jetton Avenue on Howard, lived a family of famous circus performers and high-wire trapeze artists, reputedly with the Ringling Brothers and Barnum & Bailey Circus that wintered south of Tampa in Sarasota, whose names were something like "The Zabriskies" but I can't remember...I don't think they were the Wallendas. But there was a large trapeze in their front yard and a group of us kids would troupe up to watch them practice. They did all sorts of high swinging and aerial somersaulting and ankle drops and acrobatics to our amazement. Of course, there was a very large net strung beneath them and occasionally one would miss and drop into it and bounce back up halfway—waving to us at the apogee—to our absolute elation—wishing they would let us do that, too.

CHAPTER 8

Airplanes, entertainment, & serendipity

One of the main attractions was the airport out at the end of Davis Island that nosed up to downtown Tampa, the Peter O. Knight airport (still there, by the way). Davis Island was only partially built up then so there were mostly empty lots and wooded areas. At the end out in Tampa Bay next to the airport, a cement bulkhead was rimmed with beautiful Australian Pines. Now, as I can see from Google Earth, they have been replaced by expensive homes. Right at the edge nearest the city was a country club with swimming pool and tennis courts; there was no room on the island for a golf course, I don't think—at least not adjacent to the club. We were either members or it was open to the public and I remember going to a lot of tennis matches there with both Dad and Mother. The players were always dressed in white: white short-sleeved shirts and white long pants and white tennis shoes...sometimes white sun visors but not sunglasses although I recall there were a lot of trees offering shade; sunglasses were not as popular then as now. Don Budge's name I have remembered all my life; there were no doubt other famous ones whom I must have watched but do not recall. All this did install a love for the game and in later life that was my personal sport rather than golf. I played up until I reached 80.

There was also a big swimming pool where I took swimming lessons.

Daddy Chick (I still called him that) loved airplanes. He'd take me— or the family—to airports frequently as aviation was still somewhat in its infancy. One time he took me along with him on a trip to Miami and I distinctly remember we went down to a water's edge and watched Pan American Clippers take off and land on the water. This was just before the Great Trans-Atlantic and Trans-Pacific monoplane and hull-shaped fuselage ones; these were still the old high bi-wing types with the two engines suspended on the wire struts over a boat-like hull fuselage with twin rudders perched high likewise on struts over the back end.

At the Peter O. Knight airport there was only a single north-south runway but a lot of exciting things were always going on. My Dad would take me out there almost every weekend (that I wasn't riding the trolley). He liked to hang around the hangars and I think he took some flying lessons when I was not with him. One thing he did that I never will forget was how he drank his Coca Cola from the bottle he got out of the dispenser (of course I got one, too). He would also buy a little bag of salted peanuts and drop a few into the Coke. I tried that, too, and found it good but not something I got into the habit of doing.

I remember one of the biggest events at the airport—must have been in 1937. Sixty-five (or could it have been sixteen?) U.S. Army Air Corps Boeing P-26 "Peashooter," pursuit planes landed for display to the public. These were single-seaters colored with a bright blue fuselage, bright yellow engine cowling, and bright yellow wings and tail. The wheels had blue 'pants' on them (streamlined coverings over the top halves). I knew all about them and marveled that I could touch one of them up close. (At the time, unbeknownst to the public, these airplanes were totally obsolete and a number of them were stationed in the Philippines with then Lieutenant General Douglas MacArthur's ill-fated Pilipino army and air force.)

Another time—unbeknownst to Mother—Dad arranged for me to take a ride in a little yellow Piper Cub. It was a small high-wing monoplane with tandem seating and I was in the back where I could see better. We flew all over Tampa and the environs—the thrill of a lifetime for a kid like me! (When I was 18, I soloed in a Piper Cub, did tailspins, and got quite proficient and accumulated 35 hours in several types of light aircraft before the expense of $5 and hour was given up in favor of corsages for dates I took to dances.)

But that flight was not the greatest—another was to come. Eastern Air Lines was just getting started back in the early 1930s and by 1937 it had built a "Great Silver Fleet" of the new low, mono-wing passenger airliner, the vaunted Douglas D-C3. It was a marvel of the time on a par with the new Pan-American Clipper. With much advance hype, one of the beautiful all-silver airliners landed at the Davis Island airport to give courtesy rides to all who wanted. Of course, Dad had me at almost the head of the line. Wonder of wonders—I was ushered into the glittering, gleaming airplane, tilted at an angle with its tail lower than the bigger wheels under the wings, dazzling in the bright sunlight near the terminal building—my little heart racing—and escorted to a seat...a very plush seat next to a small window. Others were also being escorted aboard. Everything was so fantastic: the newness, the smell, the design, the shape of the seats, the ceiling, the strange things right over my head, the little lights, and the safety belt. I couldn't believe I was really in a really big airplane and I was going to go up in the air in it. When the two motors cranked up and settled into their even *humm*, a beautiful lady dressed up in a neat costume began to talk to us (I have no idea what she said, I was so excited) and we began to move—and I held on to the arm rests, looking out of the window as we roared down the runway gathering incredible speed before the plane gently lifted off and we were flying!

I was enthralled. The city was much farther below than it had been in the Piper Cub and everything looked so beautiful...the distance...the water...the houses...the buildings...the green land...and we were up so near the clouds I could almost touch them. (Little could I have imagined that four years later I would meet the president of this airline who had been America's leading flying "Ace" in the war only recently passed; I had no concept of time in terms of years, it's just that the war was still being talked about like it was yesterday; we were both in the hospital recovering: me from an appendectomy and Eddie V. Rickenbacker from a terrible crash—perhaps in this very airliner? My complete story later in the Atlanta episode)

Other diversions

In that much simpler world before television and the space and digital ages, we looked to comic and "Big-Little" books (a single comic strip with a full cartoon on each of the thick 100-or-so-page book), to magazines like *Collier's, The Saturday Evening Post, Look, Liberty, Time* and a new one that debuted around 1936, *Life* magazine. I devoured each as it arrived in the mail, especially *Life*, which was chock full of pictures. There was "Pulp" fiction for men with great action-filled cover illustrations like *Doc Savage* (the only one I can remember), and, whenever I could get hold of a copy, *Popular Mechanics* magazine. They all had small advertisements in the back for things like magic, tap dancing, body building, stamp collecting, and weird devices for one thing or another; I was always intrigued and wanted to send off for some but was always deterred by Mother.

We either bought an occasional comic book for 10 cents out of our weekly allowance or simply rode our bikes (we all had junior sized 20-inch bicycles; I only got the big 26-inch wheel size when I was 14—for Christmas—a beautiful Schwinn with white-walled balloon tires) up to the corner drug store, flopped our bikes on the sidewalk and went in to the magazine rack...picked a comic and promptly sat and perused it.

Once in a while we would buy one, but if we had looked one over pretty well there was of course no need to buy it then. The kindly druggist tolerated us. And, contrary to today, our bikes would still be laying there where we left them. The drug store was on Howard at the corner of Watrous, and next to is was a "5 & Dime" store, that I always referred to as the "Ten-cent store." Then there was a shoe store, probably a Piggly Wiggly grocery, and a cleaners and something else...

The books that we were encouraged to read were *The Hardy Boys* series, the recurring *Tom Swift* series, and single ones like *Treasure Island, The Swiss Family Robinson* and a bunch of others that don't come to mind. Late afternoon radio programs were never missed: "The Shadow" (Ominous music under: "Who knows?...Henh, henh...the Shadow Knows..."), "The Inner Sanctum" (some of which scared the devil out of me!). We also ate the products advertised, like Wheaties and Ralston Purina, a substitute for oatmeal, and the chocolaty drink Ovaltine, which I threw up one day and never touched the stuff again in my entire life. I remember an ad campaign to point out the benefits of "Dextrose" (sugar) in something or other; this of course was in the primitive days before frozen dinners and concentrated orange juice, pre-cooked bacon, and a host of things we now take for granted. One thing I'll say, though, there were few overweight or obese people back then. You can see this in all the great old movies of the '30s on TV now. A lot of people did smoke cigarettes, though—but there was no cussing or vulgarity. You never heard anyone swear—only when Rhett Butler did in "Gone With the Wind" when he uttered ***damn***. Horrors!—that was like the "F" or "N" words of today. It shocked the nation. I know, when my parents laughed and discussed it they used hushed tones so we kids would not hear the word. One today cannot believe what an innocent world it was back then: there was absolutely no mention or reference to "breasts," "pregnancies," or "navels," nor were any swear words ever uttered or heard in polite society. Even the anatomical name for private body parts were never spoken either—"pee-wee" was the only one I recall—never urination; defecation? *Whazzat?*

Radio broadcasting itself was only a decade and a half old. It was AM (which nobody knew stood for "Amplitude Modulation, for the radio transmission carrier waves modulated in crests and troughs to reproduce sounds—and emitted in straight, line-of-sight waves, only as far as the horizon. "Short Wave" radio, which was an off-shoot bounced its amplitude waves way beyond the horizon off the ionosphere far above the earth and ricocheted in similar fashion all the way around the globe so could be tuned into in foreign countries.—*if* you could get through the static. (FM, frequency modulation, solved that a decade later) Many is the stormy day at the beach house when that transmission was amplified in the heavier atmosphere, so I would tune into Cuba or other strange countries, fascinated with what they might be saying.

There were two major broadcast networks, the Blue and the Red, and they were having some sort of trouble (I had surmised) with the use of copyrighted music, so there was a period when a lot of older classical music was used. I don't recall what daytime programming was like—except my grandmother's soap opera serials—and I only remember the news casts around dinner time in the evenings. Those were followed by the radio comedy shows that every family in America that had a radio tuned in to hear the raspy tones of comedian Fred Allen who wrote his own "Allen's Alley," "Fibber McGee and Molly," which always climaxed with the anticipated opening of the hall closet— ignoring Molly's warning: "Don't open that closet!"—followed of course by the sound effects of a tremendous crash of all the tightly packed things falling out onto Fibber; or, "Duffy's Tavern" that always started with the announcer saying, "Ah-ah! Don't touch that dial..." or Ed Wynn "The Fire Chief" with his zany voice; Jimmy Duranty's "Dooba-dooba-DO!" and "Umbriago!", Eddie Cantor, Joe Penner, and a bunch of others I can't recall. With the recognizable voices of other main actors like Don Ameche, Gracie Allen, "Major Bowes' Amateur Hour," announcer Milton Downes hosting the Metropolitan Opera, and all, they teased the listeners' imaginations in all manners of unseen situations, augmented by appropriate sounds effects. Those times of radio bring back clear, audible memories.

The Saturday night hour-long radio program "Your Lucky Strike Hit Parade" was one never missed. All the great Big Bands (a later term): Tommy Dorsey, Harry James, Benny Goodman, Glenn Miller, Tex Beneke, Gene Krupa, *et al.*, and the singers: Bing and Bob Crosby,

Rudy Vallee, Nelson Eddy, Janette McDonald, Ginger Rogers, Dick Powell, Diana Durbin, Hoagy Carmichael, and Kate Smith and later Jo Stafford, and again too many to cite. And, all those great songs of the '30s: "Stardust," "Smoke Gets in Your Eyes," "Tea for Two," Bob Hope's "Thanks for the Memory," Gene Autry's "Back in the Saddle," "On top of Ol' Smoky," Kate Smith's "God Bless America," Gershwin's "Summertime" from his American opera, "Porgy and Bess," and too many others to count. But just hearing them again instantly brings back mental images of those times—just like (ugh) Rock & Roll must for current generations. The sound commercials of a tobacco auctioneer rolling off his staccato pitch and always ending with: "Sold American," referring to the American Tobacco Company's slogan "Lucky Strike Means Fine Tobacco," was on everyone's lips. A naughty version of "LSMFT" was also giggled by bunches of young wags. When war came, the slogan changed to: "Lucky Strike Green Has Gone to War," referring to the fact that the green color on the package was important enough to the war effort to have been dropped for white.

One song crept in and was heard on radio before, I suppose, it was stopped. I remember hearing it. It was from a negro group of singers and went like this: "Hold tight! Hold tight! Foo-Racky-Saky—Want some **seafood,** Momma..." We kids repeated it not knowing its vulgar *double-entendre*—but suspecting it was not nice. Another universally popular negro jazz song was sung and recorded by Louis Armstrong and Benny Goodman, and even danced to by Fred Astaire: "Flat Foot Floogie with a Floy Floy." The original lyric used the word "Floozie." which in those days meant 'prostitute', and only the black society knew that 'Ploy' referred to venereal disease. One wonders whether the negro community had hoodwinked the whites and just chuckled about it to themselves. Hah! I'm just waiting now in 2014 for an African-American Jazz group to come up with a Christmas song, "Hoe, Hoe, Hoe...Santa's little helper's here"...(for those who have been away on Mars, "Hoe" is black lingo for prostitute, like "Floozie" was in the 1930s and before). With all the present vulgarity, gangsta-rap, irreverence, explicit sex, and filthy words in today's songs, I would not doubt for a minute that it would be a hit.

Syphillis and Gonorrhea were whispered but never mentioned in polite company—and we kids really weren't sure really what they were. Hard drugs were only attributed to degenerate circles. Marijuana (pot) was acknowledged and giggled about but no one knew anyone who would—or had—tried it. Opium was only in movies about the Orient. That's about all we pre-teens knew about any of this stuff; it was not endemic then as it is now. Even such jokes such as accusing someone's sister being a "thespian" brought frowns—such was the innocence—or ignorance—back then, not comprehending the cognates much less the double-entendres.

Another cute song that all kids knew and sang—at least in Tampa—was the Spanish: "La Cucaracha." We sort of knew it was about a bug (a cockroach), and we mouthed the words not quite comprehending the meanings:

> "La cucaracha, la cucaracha,
> ya no puede caminar,
> porque le falta,
> porque no tiene,
> marijuana pa' fumar."

We had an inkling that "marijuana" was something not good, but I only discerned the true meaning when I took Spanish in my freshman year in college. Had we learned the second verse, it would have been redemptive:

> Ya murió la cucaracha,
> ya la llevan a enterrar,
> entre cuatro zopilotes
> y un ratón de sacristán.
> (The cockroach just died and they take her to be buried
> among four buzzards and a rat as sacristan [priest])

Other tunes we—or *I*—would pick up were ones like "Fifteen men on a dead man's chest...Yo, ho, ho and a bottle of rum" and "Give me some men who are stout-hearted men, and I'll give you ten thousand more..." that Nelson Eddy sang manfully strutting in front of a band of burgeoning patriots in the movie "New Moon," and his "Ah, Sweet

Mystery of Life...at last I've found you..." (my Mother had piano sheet music of the song and the title of the movie it was in was in German: *Geschichten aus dem Wiener Wald*, which I figured out (Tales from the Vienna Woods) and determined to learn that language some day—despite what was going on over in Europe). "Indian Love Call" and " I'm falling in love with someone" and other spell-binding duets with Jeanette McDonald—I can still hear in my mind as I write—and tune in whenever the films are shown on TCM TV. Even at those tender ages I was deeply moved by them, and I had a little statuette on my dresser of a Canadian Mounted Policeman in his red coat, riding britches, and broad-brimmed hat just like Nelson Eddy wore as a Canadian Mounted policeman. What romantic (as in mesmerizing) fantasies those were.

Along with that figure, in my top drawer I had a tiny box with a big blob of mercury that I had found in my Dad's top drawer and had appropriated. It probably came from a broken thermometer. What I used to do was drop a dime in it and then pick it up now covered with mercury and handle it—totally ignorant—as were my parents—that the stuff was deadly. It's a wonder it did not affect my brain—or...maybe it did. We knew so little in those simple times.

There was one particular fad that I had to adopt: a new comedy team appeared in a couple of movies and on radio that captured the fancy of America: Edgar Bergen and his sidekick Charlie McCarthy who was a "Dummy." Bergen was the straight-man ventriloquist for this large hand-puppet sitting on his lap that he manipulated with his right hand working the gadgets inside the dummy's chest that animated the eyes, mouth, head-turning and arm motions. The dummy's face was a delightfully comedic one and he (it) wore a monocle on one eye. Charlie's wardrobe was varied from white tie & tails to Sherlock Holmes to a French artist's beret, etc. The advertiser-promoters first offered to the public a two dimensional cut-out Charlie McCarthy dummy with a moveable jaw; then a real 3-dimensional one was offered. *I had to have that one*! Nothing else mattered—I had to have a Charlie McCarthy dummy—nothing but that would pacify me (spoiled brat? Who? *Me*?). So, soon one appeared in the mail. It was a 'real' Charlie, all dressed up in a checkered sport coat, monocle and all, and his eyes and mouth worked just like they were supposed to. I spent hours in front of the mirror trying to "throw my voice" as the instructions explained...and I convinced myself—if no one else—that I was really projecting my voice out of Charlie's mouth. I got a lot of mileage out of that...but it, too, soon faded and ended up in the bottom of my play box.

The movies had probably the most unsuspected impact on my life: for instance, those movies about fictional college life formed my image of what that would be when I went off to college...and, indeed, I did find my first year at The University of the South (Sewanee) in 1946 just like the movies. Yale was the following year and a degree from Princeton culminated in marvelous experiences. My later Master of Fine Arts at the University of Florida was nothing like the movies, however.

Another very powerful influence on me was the 1937 movie "The Singing Marine" starring Dick Powell. I sang the words to that long afterward: "Over the Sea let's go men! We're shoving right off, Nobody knows where or when, It may be Shanghai, Fare well and Good-by, Sally and Sue, don't be blue...We'll just be gone for years and years and then—We're coming right back home again." (That marvelous image of the U.S. Marine Corps stayed with me throughout childhood and the Second World War—during my military prep school days—and I did join the Marines in 1947—ending up in cobat in three wars and retiring after 30 years as a Reserve colonel. Again, the power of media? Or, was it that later John Wayne movie, "The Sands of Iwo Jima"?—Couldn't have been as that film was made two years later.

(Would you believe? Just as I am writing this, of all things, the Turner Classic Film TV channel has scheduled The Singing Marine *for a 6:00 PM telecast. I hadn't seen that movie since it first came out, though the words to the song still come to mind. I viewed it and found that I had not remembered any of the story— just the song...and, for its time, of course, the movie was a silly romp. And, the way the actor-Marines wore and stayed in their blue dress uniforms would not pass muster today.)*

The new phenomenon on film in the '30s was the animated cartoon short. The great "Mother Goose" of the 20th Century, Walt Disney, created the early "Mickey Mouse," "Minnie Mouse," "Horace Horsecollar," "Donald Duck," and "Pluto" characters that captivated the world. After some rather crudely designed ones like "Steamboat Willie," the absolutely stunning "Three Little Pigs"—in color—was the film hit of the time; others, and, of course, the incredible "Snow White and the Seven Dwarfs" had the nation in its thrall with a lasting, fantastical visual impact, as did all the other Disney marvels. Others were produced as well by other animators; "Betty Boop, the 'Oop Girl" was one based on the alluring "Flapper" of the preceding decade of the 1920s. We kids used to mock her zany 'call': "Boop, boop, a-doop" and roll in laughter. On the more serious side was "Charlie Chan," the inscrutable and mysterious Chinese detective with his signature, "Ah, so..." And we used to chant things like, "Chink, chink, Chinaman sitting on a fence, trying to make a dollar out of fifteen cents..." Or, the more challenging: "A hundred bottles of beer on the wall and one of them fell off—then, ninety-nine bottles of beer on the wall, and..."—all the way down to zero.

Sinister actor Boris Karloff in "Frankenstein" was a scary one as was "King Kong" that astounded audiences by the animation of that giant ape climbing the Empire State building. "Lost Horizon" with Ronald Coleman tweaked the imagination. James Cagney, George Raft, and Edward G. Robinson portrayed the real gangsters of the era: Al Capone, Machine-gun Kelly *et al*. Other movie stars that dominated the decade were child star Shirley Temple whose talent and charisma charmed everyone, and the "Our Gang Comedies" with a bunch of rowdy ten year olds, one of whom wore a mechanic's cap, the cut down crown of a felt hat with a tiny brim turned back up and edged with scissors to look like a sawtooth. Somehow or other I acquired one and strutted around like a dope wearing it. For the older teens there were the adorable couple, Mickey Rooney and Judy Garland, in the "Andy Hardy" series, and other teen vocalists like Bobby Breen and Diana Durbin. Later, Judy Garland's "Over the Rainbow" from "The Wizard of Oz" topped all others.

There were other movies of that period that had real impact on an impressionable tyro like myself. But one that I would not have thought would impress me, surprised me:

In 1938, Big Buddy took me along as she drove her big Packard car for a two-week vacation up in Waynesville, North Carolina, to stay at a big tall old house with a porch around the front lined up with rocking chairs (the 'Victorian' "Ager House"). The cool, high air of the mountains was a delight as was the new and strange country world I'd never experienced before. However, the car didn't take it so well. It kept stalling out. A mechanic came to the rescue by pointing out that in higher altitudes—although these were modest Appalachians—one needed to change to 'Overdrive.' He simply pulled the knob out on the dashboard and there we were, OK again. (even big cars like my grandmother's only had about 70 horsepower back then)

The town was only a single street with stores on each side and a lone movie theater down at the end. A movie was about the only thing to do outside of attending the weekly "Square Dance" in a local barn—which was very exciting, watching all those country people whirling and twirling all dressed up in their overalls, straw hats, and fancy skirts...dancing to loud music from a bunch of what looked like farmers playing guitars, violins, harmonicas, a drum, a bucket, and a saw! It was fascinating! (Little did I know that two decades later I would be directing a Country-Western band on TV: Lester Flatt & Earl Scruggs on WSAZ-TV in West Virginia)

Anyway, my Grandmother and I would go to each new movie that came to town. She announced one titled "Pig May-lion"—and the name put me off. I didn't want to see any movie about 'pigs'. We went anyway and I noticed the marquee that spelled it "Pygmalion"—whatever that meant. (the precursor of the marvelous 1960s musical remake as "My Fair Lady" in color and with Rex Harrison and Audrey Hepburn, whose singing was dubbed in by Julie Andrews) It was an English movie (in black & white, of course, before technicolor). As I sat and watched (Leslie Howard, whose name I happened to remember, and some woman, whose I don't), I became enthralled. I had never seen a movie like this one...and it sparked something in me beyond entertainment; it had a meaning, or a lesson. And, I loved the language; it was smooth and slightly different from the way most people talked. Upshot: I came out of the theater quite pleased and prattled on to Big Buddy how good I thought it was. One thing that always endeared me to my grandmother were little things like the ubiquitous fan at her wrist, but especially in this particular theater in North Carolina where the movie-goers must have just come out of the fields and a heavy odor of straw and manure hung over the audience. Out of the corner of my eye I'd catch my sweet grandmother—*Grande Dame* that she was—gently holding her perfumed hanky to her nose throughout the movie. I can see her now doing that in the darkened theater.

Whereas Pygmalion had impressed me, "The Dawn Patrol" became my real favorite—even to this day! The 1938 remake of the 1931 movie (which I did not see) was the most perfect film 'story' I ever saw. Actor Basil Rathbone played the English flight commander of a fighter squadron in France in the World War flying French Nieuport 28 airplanes. Two of his experienced pilots were Errol Flynn and David Niven. (oddly, there was not a single female in the picture). The story hinged on Rathbone's 'weight of command' versus the rash dare-devilishness of his two top pilots and their resistance to sending up new, untrained pilot replacements too soon—and their promptly being shot down. I saw the movie several times, and, two decades later when I was operations director of another TV station—and that movie was in the station's film library—I scheduled it for on-air about every six months just so I could see—and re-live—it again.

One other unique thing that the movies had back then was always a 15-minute newsreel, like "The March of Time" that visually synopsized major national and world events. (Today that has been replaced with strings of promotionals and commercials; besides we can see news reports all day and night on TV). In 1937 a newsreel had a film sequence of Japanese airplanes attacking a U.S. Navy river gunboat, the USS *Panay,* in the Yangtze River in China on its way to investigate the earlier "Rape of Nanking" by the Japanese. I knew nothing about what was going on but recall clearly the images of the planes attacking and sinking the boat—the incident becoming a world-wide news report.

The really big one, though, that people purposely went to the movies to see in the newsreels was the horrendous explosion and crash on May 6, 1937, of the visiting German passenger Zeppelin, the "Hindenburg," as it tried to moor itself in a strong crosswind at the U.S Naval Air Station at Lakehurst, New Jersey. Lightning or static electricity caused the airship buoyed aloft by highly explosive hydrogen gas to explode in midair in a violent fireball and smoke and crash in a burning, twisted heap of aluminum and canvas, killing 35 of the 97 passengers and crew. It was an incredible sight which the still pictures in the newspapers did not convey in all its moving horror. It stunned the nation—and, of course, the Germans. The only positive thing that resulted from it was the halting of the use of hydrogen gas in lighter-than-air craft (like the barrage balloons and the Zeppelins the Germans used in WW I) and its replacement by inert helium gas (of which there is a finite amount on earth). Infrequent movie newsreels were to that time what continuing televised news is today.

My literary career launched:

It was some time during this period when we were down at the beach house; I was about nine years old. My dear grandmother was quietly typing away...probably writing another poem. When she stopped and went downstairs for some reason, I went into her bedroom and put a clean sheet of paper in the typewriter. Calliope must have been looking over my shoulder (of course I couldn't have named that Greek Muse then; I wasn't even sure what poetry was, except that the end words were supposed to rhyme).

So, I began pecking away with one finger searching for each letter key, and after a short time I came up with the following—which elicited a goodnatured laugh from Big Buddy—and began my own writing career:

<pre>
(sic)   THE THREE LITTLE PIGS
The wolf said come down from there
Ill get you before the bear
But the wolf didnt realize
That the bear was so great in size
The three pigs climbed down from the tree
While the wolf was watching a bumble bee
The wolf turned around to see them gone
And the wolf said Ill blow my horn
The pigs ran to the house
And the wolf said Ill get a mouse
The next day they went for a walk
On the road they saw the wolf writing with chalk
The wolf turned and said you pigs I will catch
The pigs were on the run when they decided
the gun they would fetch
When the pigs were home and near their doom
The smart pig pulled the trigger and there was a loud boom
The pigs saw the wolf on the ground
They said well sell his meat for twenty cents a pound
                    THE END
</pre>

Chapter 9

Horror, dummies, and enigmas

From time to time a "Fair" would come to town and everyone would go. It was a different and anticipated form of excitement. Except for a few lewd, sleazy, and obviously fraudulent runway booths, the atmosphere was wholesome, interesting, instructive, and fun. The loud organ **oom**-pah-pahs and music of the Merry-Go-Round, the Whirl-a-Gigs, Bump Cars, Ferris Wheel, cotton candy, soda pop, cheap souvenirs and such, provided background for the hawkers shouting their pitches for the Elephant Man or Bearded Lady, the smallest woman on earth, the half-man-half-beast, the strongest man, etc., etc....The one that got me, though—and I mean GOT me—was the "Lady being Sawed in Half":

Standing beside my Dad down below the 'Barker'—I was startled when the Barker eyed me and asked (my Dad) if I could join him on stage where the lady was already laid out ready to be sawed in half. Next thing I knew I was up there standing right by the lady's head with her closed eyes and wincing grimace already firmly set—and I held her hand: the Barker quickly signaled and the great big buzz-saw began its wicked deed approaching the lady's belly...when it touched her, blood and stuff began to spit off all over the place—and I froze! She WAS being sawed in half!—and I was holding her trembling hand! Frightened though I was, I held on throughout the entire ordeal, trembling a bit myself, I'm sure.

The Barker then grabbed my hand and held it up to the onlookers then pointed me back to my Dad. In the meantime, the lady had miraculously recovered and had gotten up unscathed and was bowing to the clapping audience.

I went home in stunned silence. And, I had horrible nightmares for many nights thereafter. I can still see that saw tearing through her body. Just a minor, temporary childhood trauma—*Yeah*!

Associated with nothing in particular was something I will never forget either: the eerie sounds emanating from far off in the direction of where the International Airport is now...of the German-American Bund (I was told). Evidently they gathered together—and this was in 1937 or so—to drill and march to the tune and step of a military marching band which could be clearly heard every Saturday evening. No one made any particular connection with Hitler—or that I recall anyone talking about—or thinking anything of it. I'm sure it stopped abruptly once the Germans invaded Poland in 1939. I distinctly remember seeing pictures on the front page of the newspaper showing the Nazi bombing of the free port city of Danzig. I remember asking my parents what that was all about and why did they do that? That of course was to be the beginning of a different education of a world immersed in conflict that I was to grow up in.

A whimsical rendition of a carnival I painted as a freshman in college

"Ola"

"O-de-Ola," as my sister and I affectionally called her—to her utter delight—and of all of the negro servants we had working for us, she is the only one I remember well. Ola Lucas came to us when we moved just around the corner from Watrous Avenue over on to Jetton into a larger, four-bedroom house on the corner on an oversized lot with Australian Pines and a little fish pond that was always dry between us and the next door neighbor. The garage of course was detached and the driveway faced the side street. I'm sure my parents never bought the houses we lived in; they moved so often, they must have always rented.

Ola was a stout woman of indeterminate age—to me, at least—because in childhood, what did anyone else's age matter? I was a kid and everyone else was an adult. Simple. She was kind and, I'm sure, loved my sister and me; I know we loved her. Whenever she was asked to stay over and baby-sit us, she would come up to either mine or my sister's room and we'd lie on the bed leaning back against the pillows against the headboard while she told us stories of her life. And she told such charming tales...all of them cozy and family-oriented. The way she described things, they were not too dissimilar to our own little lives. We always welcomed them. She was not particularly articulate (if I could even have articulated that word myself at that age) but she used descriptive enough language to make them real to us. I recall she used to say the word, "our," as "ow-ver." Another endearing thing she always said when she wanted to shoo us away was, "G'wane, boy—I ain't studin' you!"

Mother and Dad used to drive her home after a rather long or hard day and she would sit in the back seat with my sister and me and sort of doze leaning her head against the back window of the car. One time she came down with an infected ingrown toenail that badly needed attention. Mother and Dad had to take her somewhere for medical treatment and it took a long time to heal—especially back in those days. But we took care of her. And, we even took her on trips to Jacksonville when we vacationed at the beach house. (I immortalized her, so to speak, as a character in one of my novels later).

School Days, School Days...

The public schools I attended from First through Seventh grades were just ordinary schools of the times. And, I loved every minute of them. I couldn't wait to get to school each day. I adored each of my teachers—all nice ladies. And, I loved sitting at my desk and working or listening to the lesson or answering the teacher's questions—or being called on to write something in chalk on the black board. Or, be assigned to stay a few moments after last period to erase and clean the blackboards. The recess periods and the lunch breaks were anticipated as well. There were no fights on the playground nor ill manners in the cafeteria. Everything was so pleasant and new and challenging and fun and I just relished being there. No having to drag me off to school in the mornings.

As I mentioned, my first grade had been partly in the A.C. Moore School in Columbia and at a second school that no longer exists. In Tampa, I attended the John Gorrie Elementary School from second through 6th grades. My report cards were always satisfactory and I never got into trouble. Mistakenly, a 6th grade teacher once thought I had sassed her (oh—far from me to ever do such a thing!—) so she made me stand in the corner of the classroom—my only infraction ever. My memories are now just a blur but one thing that I recall quite well, because it had stuck with me all my life, was my learning the subjunctive mood in English in the fifth grade. Yep. In a little old ordinary grammar school in the unsophisticated—supposedly backward—1930s, I learned something like that. (For you college graduates who don't quite remember what that is: instead of using the past tense when describing something that you would have done, i.e., "If I **was** in his shoes, here's what..."; since you are **not** "in his shoes," you use the subjunctive: "If I **were** in his shoes, etc." Subjunctive in this example indicates an action that is contrary to fact: you really only conjured up the idea of being "in his shoes." See? Now go back to your Twitter.)

One of the things we had to do every day was "Penmanship." We all detested it...slanted ovals over and over...all with the arm not the wrist...then the "a's" "b's"...and on and on. Being artistic I had no problem...just boredom. Despite how much I hated the drilling over and over, I thank those dear teachers for holding fast and demanding that we learn to write a good script—just like they'd write in longhand on the blackboard. Thus, to this day, when I write something important it is in that clear and attractive hand that I was forced to learn. Thanks again, you wonderful teachers. In fact, I really did adore all of my teachers—well, except maybe one who picked the new colorful transparent plastic ruler I had just bought (all others were wooden at the time)...examined it and said that I should not have such a thing on my desk (or some lame excuse) and simply walked away with it and put it on her desk and began using it. *Grrrrr*!

We all had so many friends in school—boys and girls. More often than not, I would walk home from John Gorrie...from the corner of West De Leon, over to South Boulevard past Wilson Junior high, on down West Swann—or cut through neighborhoods—to Howard, then to Watrous and home. Of course there was much dallying along the way: a kid needing a partner to pitch to, or a time-out to swing on a big old tire swinging by rope from a stout tree branch. Or stop to chase a cat or pet a friendly puppy. Once a friend I was walking with took me into a strange place that his dad visited, a Veterans of Foreign Wars bar (I knew that was for World War soldiers), and I don't know why or what we did there but I remember a lone, bedraggled figure slumped over the bar with a beer bottle in his hand. I made no judgment—my Dad drank a beer occasionally—I just couldn't figure out why the man had to come here to do it.

Most of the time, the slow-paced walk home with book bag over a shoulder was further delayed by the presence of one of the girls walking with us reaching her house. We'd stop to chat or play or show off or anything to dally. When we did too long and reached home just before dinner...I don't know about the others, but I know I was sternly questioned. Instead of realizing my Mother's rational concern for my whereabouts, I had some disturbing idea that I was not supposed to be around girls as playmates. I think that contributed to my innate shyness that I had a hard time overcoming in later life—and of which I have been thoroughly cured for lo, these many, many decades.

One of my first loves was English princess Elizabeth. When I saw her picture—probably in *Life* magazine—I swooned. Oh, she was so beautiful...and was about my age...and wouldn't it be great for her to be my sweetheart? I 'mooned' (in the old, decent meaning of that word that meant romantically gazing at the stars and moon and dreaming chaste dreams—not today's sticking your naked butt out a car window!) It wasn't to be, naturally, but my withdrawn mood observed around the house was delicately allowed to work itself out.

Mary DuPree was an attractive classmate who a group of us boys liked to ride our bicycles over to visit many an afternoon. She lived in a very big house with giant oak trees in the front yard facing Bayshore Boulevard at the corner where Howard Boulevard dead-ends. I guess what attracted us most was those big trees. They were magnificent spreading oaks whose trunks were as large as a car and whose long, low, thick limbs stretched out so far they almost touched the ground near the street. It was not difficult to climb up and then to straddle out onto one of the limbs. When you got way out, though, the thought would clearly occur that it was really a pretty long way down to the grass...and you'd have second thoughts about continuing...then, how to turn yourself around without losing your balance and really plunging to the ground? And the limbs were too thick to hand-walk them like back at Billy Armstead's. So, you slowly bent down from the sitting position to the almost crawling one to squirm around carefully until you were facing back toward the trunk. Funny, you'd come back a week later and do the same stupid thing. The reward for all this visiting was, of course, a mid-afternoon treat from the visitée's mother...cookies, a glass of chocolate milk, or a peanut butter and jelly sandwich with an occasional Coke.

One girl in my sixth grade class I found myself kinda smitten with...in that 'puppy love' sense. Her name was Frances. Frances Cohen, and she was a bit taller than I was and I was still very shy...I don't think I even talked to her or that she even paid any attention to me—like so many sitcom literary clichés. (Funny, the same sort of thing happened several years later when I was taking a Saturday morning art class in a the art studio of Harold Hilton in downtown Jacksonville: there were some girls in the class and one was a bit taller than I, Kitty

Adams—and I was a bit shy and distant with her. To show how Fate plays funny tricks, a decade later—after college—I married her and she is the mother of our four children.)

Anyway, back to Frances Cohen: Christmas time came along and the only person I thought of giving a present to was Frances, who lived down a ways on Morrison Avenue just behind where we had moved to around the corner from Watrous to Jetton Avenue. So, when the Christmas break came and I had wrapped my present to her, I walked determinedly down Morrison to her house. I got there and, with trepidation, stepped up and rang the doorbell. Frances' mother came to the door and I gulped and meekly asked if Frances was home? She smiled indulgently and beckoned to Frances who was in the living room behind her next to the Christmas tree. I ventured in awkwardly and thrust out the present. Frances gleamed pleasantly as her mother observed amusedly and Frances introduced me as she began to unwrap the present—obviously a book. When she had done so, she held up my nice little volume entitled, "Twenty-Thousand Leagues Under the Sea" by Jules Verne—which I thought she would like—same as I would.

She thanked me profusely and I politely departed—perspiring a bit and a bit relieved—thinking that I had really done it! Really had spoken to her and she had spoken to me. I just knew she would enjoy the book; I hadn't read it but a lot of guys had said I should.

We soon moved back to Atlanta and I forgot all about Frances.

ASIDE: Thinking back, I hadn't quite realized that both "The Wizard of Oz" and "Gone With the Wind" had come out in that same year, in 1939. My memory of first seeing the "Wizard" was at the grand Florida Theater in downtown Jacksonville. That beautiful interior was all in a Spanish style and had a big blue ceiling with blinking star lights in it that were faded up and down appropriately. There was always an 'organ interlude'— eliciting un-stifled *groans* from many—between features or just before the main feature so the audience could adjust themselves comfortably, get their chatting over with, or take a bathroom break. The grand electronic organ platform would rise from one side of the orchestra pit with the organist already playing and the sound reverberating throughout the interior. Despite the audience's shuffling and talking—all things considered—it was a very pleasant interruption. Other times, a "Travelogue" short would be the breaker, and these usually received their share of bored groans as well. Despite their interest, they were corny (They are run even now nostalgically on TCM's classical movie channel on TV and are interesting insights onto what recognizable places looked like almost a century ago).

As to "GWTW," I thought that great movie premiered in Atlanta when I was living there. Although our family did not attend the grand opening at the also grandiose Fox Theater on Peachtree Street, I seemed to remember all the hype, fanfare, newspaper articles, and billboards around town.

So, how could this have been in the same year? I admit: while everything I have been writing is from my childhood memory alone, I did have to go on Google to get the exact dates these films debuted: the "Wizard," on August 25th, 1939, and "GWTW" that December— which does clear up when we moved from Tampa (via my sister and my staying in Jacksonville during the move) and our being in Atlanta for me to start Seventh Grade in September the following year, 1940.

That would make more logical my entering the eighth grade in Jacksonville in September of 1941. The idea that I was in Atlanta for the "GWTW" affair was mistaken—I must have read or seen it in the newsreels...the mis-recollections of youth.

ANOTHER ASIDE: As I write this, our two lovable dogs, a two-year old female Italian Greyhound, *Bianca la Bella Bambina*, and newly acquired Sheltie, *Laddyboy Our Utter Joy*, are cavorting around my feet.

Which brought to mind that all during my growing up, I never had a dog long enough to form an attachment to it. I had one or two but they were short-lived, succumbing either to sickness or being run over by a car.

Oddly, in my first marriage, we always had one or two dogs that fit in quite well with the four children. In my second, my wife and I have always had two: a Sheltie and an Italian Greyhound.

Never a cat.

Our lovable lap companions in 2014

The 1940s

Background:

THE DECADE OF THE 1940s was far different from the preceding one; the '30s had overall—at least in the United States—not been tranquil for most and was sluggish and difficult economically. It was plagued, too, by civil unrest like the 1932 "Bonus-Army's" civil assault on the nations' capital by 25,000 unemployed veterans from the recent Great War demanding pre-payment of a bonus scheduled them for 1945. Chief of Staff of the Army, General Douglas MacArthur and his Deputy, Colonel Dwight Eisenhower—both of whom would would head the coming war on both fronts respectively—were ordered by then President Herbert Hoover to put and end to their protest and encampment near the Capitol. It was highly suspected that communist elements had been behind their "March on Washington."

During that decade, communist infiltration had gained a foothold due to the disillusionment with Capitalism's stock market crash in

October of 1929 that took down banks, the economy, and left unemployed heads of households bereft of hope. Ignorant of what communism really was or dictator Stalin's ruthless extermination of 35 million of his people, many began thinking that that system might be preferable to America's Constitutional Republic. "Labor" (those still with jobs) threw "sit-down" strikes in factories which halted production and "walk-outs" that paralyzed others, including the automobile industries. As both labor and race riots ensued, the newly-elected president, Franklin D. Roosevelt, had inaugurated a number of governmental counter remedies that bordered on socialism: the NRA (National Recovery Act), the WPA (Works Projects Administration), the CCC (Civilian Conservation Corps), Social Security, bank prop-ups, labor favors, and paternal "Fire-side" radio chats to assuage the general public fears, as he had stated in his first inaugural address: "...the only thing we have to fear is fear itself." During the entire decade of the 1930s, all governmental efforts did little to stem the Great Depression that plagued it; it was the Imperial Japanese government that ended it when they infamously attacked the U.S. Naval Base in Hawaii that fateful Sunday morning of December 7th, 1941.

"Fateful," because, as Fate would have it, in the end it was the perpetrators who surrendered unconditionally, due to having "awakened a sleeping giant," (the U.S.), as the commander of the attack, Admiral Yamamoto, so prophetically opined following the attack that pulled America into the Second World War—and out of the Great Depression.

Two days after the president's declaring a "...state of war now exists between the United States and the Empire of Japan," the Axis Powers, Germany and Italy, declared war on the U.S. We now had a two-front war on our hands that immediately solidified the country's will to fight —tightening its belt, rapidly increasing its armed forces (from 100,000 up to 16 million) and its industrial might to incredible heights. That industrial production of "butter and bullets" had to provide for the U.S. and its Allies as well—including Communist Russia that was slowly reeling back the massive German attack that Hitler ordered shortly after conquering France in 1940 but losing the air "Battle of Britain" and aborting his plans to invade that impregnable island fortress.Typical of patriotic posters during the war years. The art on this one was done by famous illustrator Dean Cornwell.

NOTE: *Following the Korean War I had two career choices: either the local TV station or as assistant to this artist Cornwell, who had been commissioned to paint a mural and needed artistic help. As my style fitted his, I interviewed—but, fortunately, chose the former: a career in television that led to advertising, publishing, and art, as well.*

If there was one positive thing that came out of the Depression, it was the moulding of America's "Fighting Man." The Japanese soldier fought under the brutal *Bushido* warrior code to die for the Emperor no matter what, and he had no concern for human life; in short he was barbaric. The German soldier was tough, brain-washed and highly trained and ruthless—often barbaric as well. The world wondered: would the volunteer American armed forces be a match for either of these adversaries?

Astoundingly, our soldiers, sailors, and Marines whipped the pants off the enemy (although the German armies they faced in Europe were mostly battle-weary, depleted, and virtually exhausted. Our U.S. Marines in the Pacific whipped the tar out of the Japs in all battles— one-on-one as well as as a force assaulting a defending enemy, as our Navy sank the entire Japanese Imperial Navy in ferocious sea and air battles, as the Marines conquered Pacific island after island in bloody assaults, winning hard-fought victory after victory. Even the newspapers referred to the enemy as "Japs" in those politically UN-correct days. As in all wars up till then—the enemies were not coddled by sweet appellations (lest they be offended!); they were called names held over from the previous war, like Huns, Krauts, Bosch, and worse, with unmentionable adjectives describing them. Both those enemies then were tough, inhumane, often fanatic, even barbaric. But tough Americans, most of whom had hardened through the Depression, rose to the task. The U.S Army, under MacArthur plodded its way up the larger islands and recaptured the Philippines for a final joint battle for a Japanese home island, Okinawa, before tough then President Harry Truman ordered the dropping of the two Atomic bombs onto two enemy cities and the Japanese surrendered.

As they had in the First World War, the fresh American "GI" Army, Navy, and Marine corps (and their air components) fought fiercely and courageously and bested the vaunted enemy at every turn.

Thus, the first half of the decade of the 1940s would be totally consumed with the war; the second half, with disbandment and recharging the economy for peacetime. As the U.S. went to war, many common things were longer became available. Automobile plants turned to making aircraft, certain foods were rationed as was gasoline

112

to only several gallons per week for the average family, meat was rationed, margarine substituted for butter, and discarded tinfoil was collected for the "War Effort."

In the area of cultural endeavors, an art style termed "Art Deco" had had profound influence during the 1930s on the arts, architecture, sculpture, design of furniture, airplanes (especially war planes), ships, and common utensils: the racy "Chord" automobile, the neat Eastern Airliner DC-3, the New York city's Chrysler Building, WPA buildings in Washington, D.C., and other 'modern' structures and artifices nationwide. This was topped by the quintessential 1939 World's Fair in New York City with its dominant signature Art Deco structure, the Trylon and Perisphere. The Age had begun streamlining in tune with the future. All of that ceased abruptly with the advent of World War II.

There was also continuing expected sense of decorum for society. No matter how hard hit by the Depression, people dressed decently when they went out...shopping, to church, when traveling, to their clubs, etc. Neither my grandmother nor mother would dare go out without a fashionable dress and hat with veiled face net, white gloves, and collar furs if cool enough—and, of course, stockings and high heels. Hidden underneath were corsets and garter belts to hold up the stockings. Men always wore double-breasted and three-button coat suits with vests and fedora-style hats. People were polite as well; public disturbances were rare. You never heard any cursing in conversation or commerce—neither on the street nor a home. None of this, at least in my tiny sphere.

This decade of the 1940s had two parts to it: the first half was **de**structive, the second half, **con**structive. Both consumed my entire teens.

Of course, I was oblivious of such any distinction as both were my thoroughly glorious formative years.

Chapter 10

Atlanta again, then back to Jacksonville

A new adventure—*as I saw it*

Our new 1940 residence in Atlanta was an upstairs, two-bedroom apartment on NW 26th Street a little way past the junction where Spring Street joins Peachtree, then a few blocks beyond the little train station on the left. 26th Street ended in a loop at the bottom of its hill, beyond which were woods and a deep valley as far as one could see—a great area to explore.

Again, we were in a good neighborhood—modest—but safe and quiet. The mayor lived across the street and there were a few kids, one who lived in our apartment building. A little girl down the street was my sister's age (four years younger) and her name was Billie Bryant. Unbelievably, Billie later married a prep school classmate and life-long friend of mine, J.D. Henry—and we still see each other occasionally.

When school started in September, I was enrolled in O'Keefe Junior High school down close to the Coca Cola bottling plant nearer the downtown and at 10th and Techwood Drive at the northeast corner of Georgia Tech University. I guess Dad dropped me off in the morning as he drove to work downtown. I usually took the bus on Peachtree or walked home with a couple of friends. We would take a short cut across the large open athletic field in front of the two-story school building itself. (Today, that whole field and the surrounding area is that deep paved canyon with the dozen or so lanes of constant streams of vehicular traffic negotiating Interstate 75. The streets that we crossed—10th, 8th, and Ponce de Leon—are now bridges and intricate over- and under-passes.) When we leisurely strolled home in mid-afternoon either up Spring or Peachtree, there was hardly any traffic and it was mostly open space with a few low buildings here and there. Many is the time I rode my junior-sized bicycle all over that area, including up to Ponce de Leon, on both the streets and sidewalks. (Peachtree was a far cry from the narrow, congested, impeded, roadway in the valley of the giant skyscrapers that it is nowadays.)

Seventh grade during the first semester in that school was pretty exciting. It was the largest school I had ever attended, and junior high had a lot of things my elementary's did not have, like an "art" program, in which I excelled. The teacher often thumb-tacked my drawings up on the board for all to see. I did pretty well in all the other classes, too.

This was the first time I experienced peer pressure to some degree, too. The vogue then was for guys to turn up the cuffs of their long pants three folds to expose their socks, and to turn up the cuffs of their long sleeves likewise. It made us "cool" or something (although that word did not come into use until later during the war). The music program also appealed to me; there was an orchestra and a marching band. I wanted to play the trumpet because that was like the bugle I had earlier acquired somewhere along the line and on which I had taught myself to play 'Taps' and 'Reveille'. I guess there were too many others who thought that would be a popular instrument, too, because there were no more openings; so, the instructor convinced me to take up the French horn. The instrument he handed me was not exactly a French horn but an 'Alto horn' that looked somewhat like it and the fingering was the same. So that is what I started to learn. We were allowed to take the instruments home to practice and so I did, lugging the thing in its big black case on the bus a couple of afternoons a week. My mother, however, didn't 'cotton' (as they say down South) to the idea; she thought that at my age of eleven and still growing that blowing through the mouthpiece would affect the growth of my lips and jaw (as it was, my chin was a little underdeveloped)—and she didn't want me ending up like the cartoon character of the day, "Andy Gump" who was chinless and rater stupid looking. She was right, of course, and it might have been that year that I was started on upper and lower braces to which I had to attach tiny rubber bands and wear them all day and night in order to force my jaw to develop normally—for which I am eternally thankful that she persisted.

So, right away—after inadvertently putting a dent in the horn—I switched to the drum—a nice-sized marching drum with snares. As if my vain attempts at learning the scales on the horn had not annoyed the family and neighbors, my coming off the bus and marching down 26th Street to my accompanying drum beat was something that, I guess, the men-folk who worked during the day escaped but heard about from their wives when they came home.

Dangerous adventures

As boys of that age are wont to do, a couple of us would venture into the woods at the foot of the street down the steep incline to an enormous pipe that spanned the valley. It was so big and round that you easily—but very, very carefully—could walk out on it. Out a few yards or so, though, one slip and you were a "goner"! The slope below was quite precipitous and the rocks and bushes would have ripped you to pieces. Thankfully, we had the good sense not to show off or do something completely that stupid. But it was an adventure-land right smack in the city. (Today, that complete area is now the northern fork of I-75, the natural valley having lent itself to the configuration of the all-paved Interstate)

Another episode that we kids did not consider 'dangerous'—but our downstairs neighbor did—was the night were were playing outdoors and decided to bang on the neighbor's front door—and run!

We sneaked up, opened the common door to the apartments, then stealthily stepped over and banged the heck out of the neighbor's front door. Instead of the neighbor's expected opening and peeking out and figuring it was just the kids—this man came running out and chased us! He recognized who we were, grabbed me, and hauled me up the stairs to my parents—who were shocked at my reported behavior, apologized to the neighbor and sent me to my room for further dealing with. I heard the neighbor tell them breathlessly that he had to be on guard because he was a naval reserve officer and was working on some secret things and he at first thought the intrusion might have had something to do with that.

I had no idea that anybody in our country—especially a neighbor—would be thinking or working on anything connected with the military —or war. I had caught bits of my parents' conversations and things in the newspapers and on radio but I never made the connections. I did know that the year before, the Germans had invaded Poland—and that France had just surrendered and the air Battle of Britain was being fought—and that mean ol' Hitler was stirring up more trouble. But I still didn't see how that affected us.

A new interest: model airplanes

Although I was as gregarious as the next kid, I was also content as a 'loner'. I could always occupy myself with something interesting. I don't remember how it came about but my interest in model airplanes peaked. Of course I had those vivid memories of Davis Island in Tampa. Perhaps it was the newsreels or the advertisements or magazine articles about aviation's latest developments, pictures of the amazing British Spitfires fighting the NAZI Messerschmitts, or simply the barn-stormers, or the famous air races. Of course I knew about Lindbergh's trans-Atlantic flight—and the kidnapping of the baby—but there had also been constant stories about Will Rogers' and Wiley Post's around-the-world flights, Amelia Earheart's ill-fated one, and many about the air races of those experimental times. The names of Rosco Turner, Jimmy Doolittle (whose name would come to prominence again two years later in his famous air raid on Tokyo), and Jacquelin Cochran rolled off my lips like those of the airplanes of the times (Thanks again Sandy Brian and Dad). So, in a store one time (I guess), I must have asked Mother to buy me a model airplane kit to build it by myself.

Late afternoon in the Fall as it got dark earlier was the perfect time for me to come in and settle down, not necessarily to do homework—I could do that after supper. But at 5:00 PM all the kid's radio serials came on: the afore-mentioned "Terry and the Pirates," "Jack Armstrong, the All-American Boy" (opening jingle): "Wave the flag for Hudson High, boys, Show them how we stand, Ever shall our boys be champions, Known throughout the land—So, Just Buy Wheaties, the Best Breakfast Food in the Land!" Talk about the power of advertising: of course we had Wheaties for breakfast while I gazed admiringly at the big pictures of Tarzan (actor Johnny Weissmuller), Babe Ruth, and whoever else was on the box—(and here I am at 86 remembering these and others!) "Terry and the Pirates": *Gong* sound effect and phonetic Chinese: "Hyiow ting, pada-roo , Dada-ah, PA—rah......T e r r y and the P i r a t e s!—*Gonnnng!*," and "The Lone Ranger and Tonto" (later discovered as the Spanish word for 'fool') "Hi-Yo, Silver...Away..." to the strains of Rossini's William Tell Overture and Lizts' *Les Préludes* (which I researched much later), "Superman." and others. That was my "quiet time" when I could build the model airplanes while listening to the radio. By sheer luck I had found, too, a wonderful model and craft store in downtown Atlanta where I could buy all sorts of needed supplies, especially that trusty banana-oil glue. I commented to the manager when I first went in that it was the best store I had ever seen, and he generously gave me a tube of glue or something, thus cementing a customer relationship.

I have no record of or precise memory of the types or how many models I built, but there were quite a few and I kept myself very busy. I think I carved a British Spitfire out of balsa wood because I remember mixing from the three primary colors red, yellow, and blue available in tiny bottles that were called "airplane dope" and was pleased to get the desired shade of brown for the camouflage by mixing all three colors. I might have made an American Curtis P-40 "Flying Tiger" fighter, too.

Not related to anything in particular, but there were new things coming on the market all the time, even though people kept saying that the Depression was not over yet. The government's NRA, or National

Recovery Act, had been knocked down by the Supreme Court, but the CCC, the Civilian Conservation Corps, was evidently successful in providing jobs, as was the Hoover Dam in Nevada, and the Tennessee Valley Authority that brought electricity to the destitute areas of Apalachia. There had been a lot of labor unrest, even movies about that; one that I had seen that disturbed me greatly was "Black Legion."

On a better note, one new product I will never forget was a new tooth paste called "Teel." It was a beautiful turquoise color and tasted great.

Also, interesting things were happening all the time. Up Peachtree Street a few blocks from us was a big, somewhat dilapidated Ante-Bellum mansion with stately columns in front just like in GWTW. Well, one day as we were driving up possibly to Buckhead, there was a major road block at the mansion: fire engines, police cars with single flashings light on top (they were not the specialized vehicles with all their paraphernalia of today's cop cars), firemen standing by with hoses—and a bunch of men in overalls in the front yard and visible inside the open doors hacking away with axes at casks of *whisky*! The strong smell and the flow of mahogany liquid draining into the street and down the gutter was quite a sight. The authorities had simply busted an illegal moon-shine operation. Occasionally an onlooker—rather down-and-out-looking—would try to scoop up some of the booze flowing in the gutter. I, of course, was intrigued and watched intently as we slowly drove by wondering why all the fuss?

Moving again—this time nearby

For some reason not deemed necessary to inform me of, we moved about a mile farther up and off Peachtree into a very charming neighborhood called "Brighton Terrace" and on one of its streets named "Brighton Road." The reason could have been that some close friends of my parents, Hix Green, Sr., whose wife, Bertha, was a second cousin of my mother's, and a house across from them that was for rent. Perhaps he had alerted Dad that it was available and it was a quite a bit more desirable than the 26th Street apartment, especially for my

Mother who could now have afternoon bridge games in a more proper setting and equate socially in the prestigious Junior League of Atlanta.

The beautiful two-story house was perched on a steep incline which made the driveway perilous in bad weather. I think there were only three bedrooms and I had the one on the back facing a large wooded area—another adventure possibility. It was a nicely wooded area with no low foliage, only leaves. We kids occasionally dug up 'Minnie" balls, calcified .50 and .67-caliber lead bullets from the Civil War ("War Between the States,"...to all you Yankees, *Suh*!)

With that move, I was transferred for my second semester to E. River's School farther up Peachtree just past Peachtree Creek, where a significant skirmish had taken place during the past "Un-pleasantness" (another reference to the War Between the States) and where I remember on the right just before the bridge there was a "Pig 'n Whistle" drive-in restaurant.

I adored E. Rivers as well. I seem to recall that there were lower grades there and none higher than the seventh; therefore, it must have been an elementary school rather than a bonafide junior high. Anyway, it was, I thought, better and more friendly than O'Keefe Jr. High that I had just transferred from. Miss Brim, was my homeroom teacher. The only class I did not particularly care for was the music class when we had to sing. I never could carry a tune—even though I loved music, especially the classics, as I have pointed out. But there was one absolutely stupid song I still hate; it went, "Dainty dancer, gaily now, step by step, lightly as a feather..."! It is probably a classic or from Shakespeare—but I loathed it!

There was a playing field on a lower flood plane next to Peachtree Creek where we played all sorts of games, mostly at that time of the season, baseball.

My cousin, Hix Green, junior, across the street on Brighton Road was my same age and we became close buddies (his father, Hix Green, Sr., owned a big automobile dealership). There were other kids in the neighborhood, including my next-door neighbor, Bill Erb (I haven't thought of these names in ages—it's amazing that they are coming back to me; pre-senility, I guess). Down the street was Billy Campbell (I wonder if he turned out to be one of Atlanta's later mayors by the same name?). Bill Erb and I had a similar interest in the Boy Scouts, each being only eleven and too young yet to join. But, we had bought ourselves the marvelous Boy Scout Manuals, and I think I memorized mine—I read and pondered over it so much. I finally joined a Troop at the Trinity Episcopal Church at the corner of Spring and Ponce de Leon which we attended.

The day I first wore my uniform—with its broad brimmed hat just like the Canadian Mounties, except in olive drab—to the meeting was a high point. I loved all the activities and the merit badges we had to earn; in effect we were competing against ourselves while also benefitting from group activities. It was great fun. One activity was 'camping and cooking'—out in the woods. So, one evening the troop was taken out to a remote spot on a promontory where you could see in the distance the skyline of the city to our south...and we had to make a little clearing to build a fire by scooping away the leaves. Then we broke out our eating utensils and frying pan and the Scoutmaster slopped a piece of meant into it and began to cook it over the small flames. As it was early Fall, it turned dark fast and we had not brought any flashlights—or not enough for us to see what we were doing. I remained quiet but thought the whole thing ridiculous. Why go to all this trouble and stumble around in the dark—then try to eat something that was, frankly, inedible? Thinking back on our campsite location, it must now be smothered under tall buildings and intertwining roadways.

For my promotion from Tenderfoot to Second Class (which my father had achieved back before the World War and had given me his badge), I had to pass the test for first aid. The Scoutmaster took me aside to administer the questions to see if I knew the material. The first thing he asked me what would I do if I cut my finger and it started to bleed. I responded just what my Mother always did—not what the manual said: "I'd hold it under the kitchen faucet and turn the water on to wash away the blood." Well, that wasn't the correct answer and I never made it to Second Class.

Even though my tenure as a Boy Scout was short, I still can recite at moment's notice the Scout Oath and Laws. To beat that, one of my later career jobs was as a top executive at the Boy Scout National Headquarters where I ran the Audio-visual department that included film, photography, museums, and the Norman Rockwell collection of 42 paintings he did on Boy Scout themes.

In our garage I tried to construct a "Soap Box Derby" racer using the tires off a baby carriage. I built a cumbersome base structure out of wood, made the front axle steerable with my feet, and had a rope tied to it to steady myself. The steep driveway was the race course and I had to have someone at the bottom on the street to give me the "go-ahead" so I wouldn't be hit by a car. It never worked like I had envisioned.

My Dad had a 1900 model Savage single-shot .22 octagonal-barreled rifle in his closet that as a kid he had pinged around with growing up in Birmingham. Of course I had been shooting BB guns since I was about six and I had taken to heart his admonition to "always look beyond your target." So, I often took his .22 out to play with—and told him about it. (he gave it to me when I turned twelve) I came across a few .22 shells in his top dresser drawer that did not seem to have bullet noses but wadded paper—so, I assumed they were blanks. Thereupon, I took them and the gun out in the back yard—with my little sister at my heels—and I told her I was going to shoot these harmless shots...and I wanted for her to stand against the tree and promised her she wouldn't feel a thing. Fortunately, some guardian angel or nagging doubt from my inner not-yet completely formed brain cautioned me to try it first at the tree—just to check it out. So, I did—with my sister looking on—and *Whap!*—some of the bark flew off the tree trunk right where I had aimed! That made me abandon my "William Tell"—so-to-speak—project and go off and shoot the rest of the *blanks* over the back fence into the woods. "Gulp!"—a close call, that I shuddered about for a long time.

Despite all the other things that kept me busy—reading the Scout manual, playing with friends, I still found time to make model airplanes while listening to the later afternoon radio serials. I made several solid balsa wood types where the kit would have a simple outline pattern for each element from which to work and a solid block of soft balsa wood to carve out the fuselage (body) and several smaller, thin ones to carve for the wings and tail surfaces. There were also tiny wheels to make struts to attach to. Onto the block the side profile of the fuselage had to be traced and the excess carved away; then the top profile and its excess carved away. With that done, you had to cut away the sharp edges and make the fuselage's edges rounded and then sandpapered them smooth. The same thing had to be done with the single, long upper wing and the two smaller lower wings; their shapes with their rounded tips had to be cut out of the thiner rectangular pieces, and then they would have to be sanded to the airfoil shape of the wings. This all took many—happy—hours. When everything was finished and conformed exactly to the plans, all of the elements would have to be carefully glued together, one piece at a time with utmost care. When one piece was thoroughly dried, the next would be applied to it. After a few days to this, the little airplane model would have been put together—all unpainted. That was the next step. Usually included in the model kit were small bottles of the required special paint. So, carefully and laboriously—and delightedly—the appropriate color would be applied to each surface of the fragile model. When all done—and perhaps smoothed a little more with a finer sandpaper, the markings would be painted on—yes, there were no easy decals to wet and stick on back then—you had to carefully paint the white star-with-red circle in its center—in a blue circle, the insignia of U.S. military aircraft. The procedure was a far cry from today's silly plastic snap-together model airplanes, ships, rockets, and such that take no ability or talent whatsoever to put together. Thankfully, I learned to make them the hard way because that was a real time of learning. Later, when I taught at the University of Florida and the class had to build some TV sets, only one other faculty member and I could build them; the students (this was 1956) didn't know even how to start and had to be shown even how to drive a nail! The other faculty member and I discovered that we had built model airplanes as described above—none of the students had.

The last model I made before the following incident (below) was a Curtis "Goshhawk" bi-wing U.S. Navy fighter plane. I was quite proud of it.

An accident leads to
an amazing encounter

Kids do a lot of dumb things—and I wasn't immune. Inside our house between the living room and the kitchen was a staircase leading upstairs. A portion of it had a bannister that ended in a curve above the bottom step. Unable to resist, I used to bend over the rail and slide down on my belly just for fun. That fun stopped abruptly one day when something didn't feel right after I got off. My stomach hurt like the dickens.

I told my mother and she felt my stomach area to my "ouches" and called the doctor, who quickly diagnosed it as a ruptured appendix. The next thing I knew, I was lying in the back seat of the car, moaning, with my head in her lap on our way to the Piedmont Hospital downtown (The Piedmont Hospital has since moved to Peachtree at the head of our Brighton Road, which would have been infinitely more convenient —but might not have ended with my amazing story), to wit: I knew that one of my heroes, World War flying "Ace," Captain Eddie Rickenbacker, had been hospitalized in Atlanta since his earlier airliner crash at the local airport. Like every kid then, I knew all about his heroics during the war and was dying to meet him. So, when I came back from surgery and awoke, I implored one of the nurses to wheel me in to meet him.

She did so, and, as they say, the rest is history:

In 2011, I wrote of this episode in a feature article for the Atlanta Journal & Constitution *in commemoration of the 60th Anniversary of the crash:*

An Indestructible Hero: Eddie Rickenbacker's crash

Eastern Air Lines' Flight 21 lifted off the Newark airfield on schedule at 7:10 PM on February 26, 1941. The new twin-engine, low mono-wing, gleaming aluminum Douglas DC-3, one of ten new 21-passenger airliners in the fledgling Great Silver Fleet, was headed to Brownsville, Texas, via Washington, Atlanta, Birmingham, New Orleans, and Houston. One of the sixteen passengers on board was 51-year old Edward Vernon Rickenbacker, president of the airline, headed for a meeting in Birmingham.

As the flight approached Chandler Field southwest of Atlanta a violent storm had the airport socked in. In the pitch black darkness in driving rain and gale-like wind, the pilots routinely over-flew the only runway to make a 180-degree turn for their final approach by radio beam back down the runway (in those early days of developing technology), not realizing that a faulty altimeter indicated the plane was a thousand feet higher than it actually was. Abruptly the craft's wings began clipping treetops short of the runway, somersaulting the shiny craft, crashing it through branches and tree trunks onto the soggy ground. Only the quick thinking of the pilot, who cut off the ignition, saved it from becoming a blazing inferno; aviation fuel soaked the horrendously twisted, mangled wreckage, the split-in-two upside-down fuselage, the broken wings, and bits and parts strewn all about.

Eerie silence. Then groans of the injured growing into agonized cries of pain.

Fighting off death again

President Rickenbacker, who had been moving toward the rear as the crash was imminent, ended up pinned between parts of the wreckage over the dead body of the flight steward who had been sitting next to him. Dazed, he began to realize that his left hip socket was crushed and a major nerve must have been severed as there was no feeling; both sides of his pelvis and left knee were broken, several ribs also—two jutting through his

Rickenbacker's crash Feb. 26, 1941 at Atlanta

skin. His left elbow was also broken, leaving the hand paralyzed, and there was a dent in his skull where it was jammed between two plates of the bulkhead.

When he overcame the initial shock, he realized he was soaking wet with blood and high-octane gasoline. Slowly he began trying to free his right hand and arm, which had escaped injury. Twisting his head slightly, a jutting piece of metal gouged his left eyeball out of its socket, leaving it dangling on his cheek. In excruciating pain, Rickenbacker mentally fought off the tranquilizing creep of pending death, willing his mind to stay awake and alive. His mettle had been tested in near-death situations before.

As creator and president of the airline he had pioneered so strenuously to build, his thoughts turned then to the nine survivors, yelling for them to report their statuses and apologizing to all for the crash—the first in the airlines' history. Continually, he shouted encouragements for them to hang on and organized those ambulatory to spread out in a box formation within shouting distance to try to find help or where they were—and to have faith that they would be rescued.

Tortuous rescue

It took over five hours for the rescue team to find the crash site. Rickenbacker shouted frantically to them to douse their kerosene lanterns lest the whole area go up in flames. News flashed locally and nationally via radio and newspaper "Extras." Especially concerned was his close friend, Ralph McGill, publisher of the *Atlanta Constitution*, which covered his recuperation in detail. Rickenbacker was a national celebrity—and one of America's best known and highly decorated World War I heroes.

Hero Aviator

As a seventh-grader in Atlanta at the time at E. Rivers School out NW Peachtree, even I knew all about Captain Rickenbacker —every kid back then did.

We grew up on the heroes of that Great War some twenty years earlier. I knew "Captain Eddie" had been Americas' leading flying ace; Medal of Honor winner to boot. We all knew, too, what that aerial fighting was like thanks to the 1938 movie, "Dawn Patrol," starring Errol Flynn, Basil Rathbone, and David Niven. I had lived that movie over and over, vicariously shooting Fokkers and Albatrosses out of the sky along with Flynn and Capt. Eddie long before Snoopy did. To

Capt Eddie Rickenbacker, 1918

127

this day I have a video of the film and view it frequently.

We kids were as concerned as anyone reading those distressing headlines. I knew my hero had officially downed, one-on-one, 26 German airplanes and balloons. Although a nationally known race-car driver before the war, he had had a rough time trying to become a pilot in the Army Air Service of the American Expeditionary Force (AEF) in France.

Aviation was in its infancy; heavier than air flying machines invented only fifteen years earlier. His determination, though, landed him flying a French-made Nieuport bi-wing fighter plane with the American 94th Aero Squadron. In one of his first aerial dogfights, Rickenbacker dived his fragile Nieuport toward an enemy plane at an astonishing speed of over 150 miles per hour —and the fabric covering of the top wing ripped off, forcing his little craft into a tailspin. Allied pilots at that time had no parachutes, so the neophyte lieutenant's only option was to tenderly nurse the small remaining lift of the lower wings at full throttle back to the aerodrome—which he did masterfully.

When the superior SPAD S.XIIIs replaced the iffy Nieuports, the 94th 'Hat-in-the-Ring' Aero Pursuit Squadron really took off. Flying these against the heretofore superior Fokker D-7s and tri-winged D-8s, the 94th racked up the top tally of enemy planes and observation balloons destroyed. It had also been the first American squadron to down an enemy aircraft and was also the last. As America's leading ace by early fall of 1918, Captain Rickenbacker took over as squadron leader.

On the announcement of the Armistice that November 11th, Capt. Eddie flew his SPAD low over the front lines, dipping his wings to cheers from the trenches below. It was a far cry from his automobile-racing career just before the war. After the war, though, he went back and bought the Indianapolis Speedway, then formed a company to build the cars he designed, before creating one of the largest U.S. airlines in the 1930s.

A Nation holding its breath

The crash site rescue was front page for days. First reports were that Rickenbacker had died. Then, learning of his heroic example before rescue, the Press extolled him even more. For ten days, though, he lay at the brink of death in (the old) Piedmont hospital in downtown Atlanta; then six weeks in a cast. Four months in all. Fortunately, a doctor was able to reinsert his eyeball, patch it, and his 20-20 vision was restored.

An acute case of appendicitis put me in that same hospital two months after the crash. My begging the nurses to wheel me in to meet him worked, and, indeed, on April 15th, I looked upon that unmistakable face smiling—supinely—out of a mummy-like cast from chin to elevated toes.

As men of greatness are wont to do, he greeted this young admirer with charm, grace, warmth, and the attention he would have one of his fellow pilots. At least, that was my naïve impression. I had brought him a gift I had made, a balsa wood model of a bi-wing Curtiss Goshawk airplane. He accepted it graciously (and, I trust, passed it on to the children's' ward) and invited me to come back the following week.

Of course I did and this time he had a gift for me: an autographed copy of the book he wrote following the war, *Fighting the Flying Circus*. The thrill of any kid's lifetime!

I still have that book—only by a sequence of its inadvertently ending up in a used bookstore in Florida—and my miraculously retrieving it years later. I reread it recently and it still stirs awe and excitement.

A third extraordinary escape from death

Shortly after WW II, I met Rickenbacker again at a lecture. Early in the war on a volunteer mission for the War Department, he had been in an Army Air Corps B-17 that crashed in the uncharted South Pacific, and he and six survivors were adrift at sea in two-man life rafts for 23 days. A solitary seagull had perched on Rickenbacker's head, which he was able to catch; that and rain water they caught in the rafts were their only sustenance. Again an American hero, he inspired those with him to hang on and they miraculously survived.

Rickenbacker then went on to further fame, creatng and guiding Eastern Air Lines up until he retired and died in 1973. Eastern Air Lines was bought by Continental in 1958 and liquidated by it in 1991, ending an illustrious 55-year history.

Presently in the Air & Space Museum on the Mall in this Nation's Capital hangs one of the original D-C3s of Eastern Air Line's "Great Silver Fleet." I often wonder—if it wasn't the one Rickenbacker crashed in—could this one hanging up there be the one I took that courtesy ride in back in Tampa? I'll never know (but I'm proud to have had six of my own aviation paintings that I did for the Marine Corps on display in an adjoining gallery in that very museum all of 2013).

I had to recuperate for some time after the appendectomy, meaning take it easy...and I had to resist temptation and simply look on and not engage in the ball games at recess time a E. Rivers. I will never forget, either, the "Fire Drills": on the exterior of the building were these enormous tubes (as big as the utility pipes spanning the valley that we were afraid to cross). They were fire escape chutes. Therefore, we did not mind at all when fire drill time came around—we thrilled sliding ourselves down these chutes...too bad there was not water at the bottom instead of grass and gravel.

Often I'd walk home from school; it wasn't all that far...dallying of course along the way. There was a grocery store just past the Pig'n Whistle on the other side of Peachtree Creek and one day I spotted an exciting poster in its window, asking for donations to British War Relief—or something of the sort. The graphic was a terrific illustration of a British amphibious airplane 'landing' on the turbulent ocean to rescue the survivors of a sinking ship. "I must have it!" So— unabashedly—I entered and went up to the man at the counter and asked for it. Surprisingly, he told me to go ahead and take it. Once home, I immediately tacked it up on my wall.

And, thus, began a collection of art, photos, and other visuals of interest that adorned the walls of my work-bed room from then throughout the following decade (until they were slowly replaced by *Esquire* magazine "Petty Girl" pin-ups when I turned sixteen and my priorities changed).

At least once a week Hix, Bill, Billy, and I would manage to visit the drug store up on Peachtree in a little strip mall at the south corner of Brighton (the term 'strip mall' hadn't been coined back then so it was just 'up to the stores' for us). Our self-treat was an ice cream soda. The drug store was right out of a Norman Rockwell "Saturday Evening Post" cover (with which we were all familiar throughout the '30s): the 'Soda Jerk"—the older kid who 'jerked' the sodas and scooped the ice cream and concocted the banana splits was behind the counter, little white cap angled jauntily. Everything was glitz, mirrors, rows of glasses and banana split dishes, candies, and other do-dads. He'd first squirt the fizz water in a tall Soda glass that bulged at the top, then a scoop (maybe even two) of vanilla ice cream into it and top it with whipped cream. We'd be sitting on the wire-backed stools along the counter in lip-smacking anticipation. It tasted soooo good! Stretching the pleasure out as long as we could, we'd drop our dimes on the counter and, of course, then go over to the magazine rack and check out the comic books and sneak a peek a the latest Esquire men's magazine for pictures of risqué, lightly clad women drawn by the artist known to all at the time as, 'Petty'. His "Petty Girls" were the closest to scandalous that there was (to us) in those innocent days (something like 'Playboy' back then would have been purged and the store burned down, most likely).

Prepping another move

That following decade of the 1940s had started out very auspiciously. I don't know what it was about my Dad's job but I think he and my mother came to the conclusion—augmented by my grandparents' urgings—that he would do better by changing jobs—especially by taking over the family business. My grandfather, "Daddy Avery," was nearing 66 years old and had no one to pass the Union Terminal Warehouse business on to, so "Daddy Chick" was the likely candidate—and a very great opportunity for him, without doubt. So, I overheard talk about that and, of course, figured that would involve another move.

It was well into the summer of 1941 when it was announced to me that I was to move back to Jacksonville and live with my grandparents until the Chenoweths could move down there as well. My sister would remain in school at E. Rivers.

Off to a military adventure, starting in the eighth grade at The Bolles School, a military academy prep school in Jacksonville, Florida, 1941

Chapter 11

So, back to Jacksonville I go—
but now to a military school

Sending me then into the eighth grade at The Bolles School, a boys' military prep school in South Jacksonville, was an idea that readily appealed to me. During the earlier times I had spent in Jacksonville with my grandparents, we would often take Sunday afternoon drives over the Acosta bridge to South Jacksonville and out the San Jose Boulevard to the school to watch the cadets parade in their smart uniforms to the stirring sounds of their own marching band. So, I knew what it would be like and ate the idea up with relish (no mustard or sauerkraut, please!).

By September of 1941, my grandparents had moved from their big house on Lomax Street in Riverside, across the St. Johns River to a new Southside development called San Marco and had constructed a beautiful new house right on the water front. This was better for my grandfather because it shortened his drive to the Warehouse just across the river now—and ideal for me because it was closer to Bolles School. The school bus stopped just up the corner from their house.

The house was two stories and brick. It faced the river with a large front lawn and some palm trees. On both sides and the back along the street—except for the double driveway—was a four-foot high brick wall.

I think both the house and the wall were painted white; I know later my grandmother had it repainted pink. Inside, it was quite spacious and light and airy. A big wide hallway went from the front door on the street right through the house to the big porch facing the river—a marvelous view across about a mile of the big bend in the river to the opposite side at Ortega. There was even a short cypress boarded dock that ended in a "Tee" with a railing and benches around it. Many were the pleasant evenings spent out there with my grandparents watching the sun set, like back on the porch on Lomax street. (For the record, I found out much later that this lovely big brick house cost $39,000 to build in 1939; today it would sell for over a million!)

The new neighborhood was great. More open, some newer homes and some older magnificent mansions of the wealthy who had moved there during the real estate boom of the 1920s: the Swishers of King Edward Cigar Company, and farther out, the famed Alfred I. DuPonts. Newer residents were the next door architect Saxby, who had designed this house of my grandparents' and the opulent, Spanish-style "San José" resort hotel at the end of the Florida real estate boom that operated just three years before it went bankrupt when the Depression hit. When that occurred, Mrs. Agnes Painter, a noted Jacksonville business woman, was holding the mortgage on it and thus acquired the property in receivership. She and her husband turned it right away into a boys military academy that became The Bolles School to which I was headed. On the left a door or two on the other side, were the Davis' who had created the Winn-Dixie grocery chain. Their son, Bobby, and I became the best of friends, as did another of my Bolles classmates, Charlie Krueger up the road. The well-kept neighborhood with its shaded streets and lovely houses was a delight to ride one's bicycle around.

A few blocks away was the commercial center at the junctions of San Jose Boulevard that paralleled the river beyond the DuPonts and Bolles all the way down past the orange groves of Mandarin and on to St. Augustine; the other was Beach Boulevard that branched off directly east and led twenty miles down to the beaches. On one side of the San Marco center was a strip of stores: a drug store, barbershop, grocery, and a few others. There was also a building that had a huge stage where many local amateur productions were performed. There was one young local girl just bubbling with talent and she became a noted attraction in any play she was in. Her name was Wanda Hendrix; everyone predicted she would make it big in Hollywood—but somewhere along the line she simply faded away. Never heard from her again. My Dad was in one play I remember: "A Bell for Adano," about restoring a destroyed bell to a Sicilian town during World War II.

Cadet Chenoweth, The Bolles School

I can hardly express my excitement upon entering Bolles at registration and getting all decked out in my first cadet uniform, the everyday one: the light gray long pants with the dark stripe down the outside of each leg, the gray long-sleeved shirt and black necktie, the shiny gold belt buckle (which we had to polish daily for inspection) on the black web belt, the black shoes (that we also had to polish every day for inspection), and the *pièce-de-résistance*, the smart, gray and black trimmed, military, 'fore-and-aft' cap with the "Bolles" insignia. That beat everything I could have imagined: the pirate, the Cub Scout, Tom

Mix, the Boy Scout uniform,—and even the imagined 'Frank Buck' outfit.

The structured military routine took some adjusting to, especially after the easy-going pubic school experiences. I was in the eighth grade, the bottom of the Junior School, which was formed into its separate company of three squads and we had to line up exactly so each time—and do that every time a formation was called for—which was for every activity: class attendance, inspection, lunch, after class programs, and athletics. For the slightest infraction of the rules and regulations, a 'demerit' was recorded. If you accumulated too many, you had to "walk them off in the Bull Ring," which meant marching with your assigned, real 8-pound, model 1903 Springfield rifle properly positioned on your right shoulder and march around the long double, divided entrance roads that led to the main school buildings—maybe five times around for each demerit—and in the broiling sun. It was a punishment, therefore, most tried to avoid. Well, yours truly, had to learn the hard way.

One of my classmates, Hugh Powell (a life-long friend as well), and I were ordered to the Bull Ring a number of times and we were about to earn reputations as trouble-makers—until a remarkable thing happened. The headmaster, Lieutenant Colonel (Florida Militia) Roger Painter (co-founder of the school with his wife, Agnes) was a wise man (though with not even a college degree—which few had back then). He called me into his office—and I mumbled to myself, "What did I do now?" He greeted me politely and told me to sit down in the chair in front of his desk. He then reviewed my academic and behavior (the demerits) records and looked me straight in the eye and asked me this question: "Avery, you are a smart young boy...your grades are tops...why do you act this way?" I don't remember what I mumbled back but those words bored deep into me. I had no answer. But, I changed at that very moment! And, for the rest of my four years at the school I never got another demerit; to the contrary, I won medals for best-drilled (manual-of-arms) cadet in both the junior and senior schools, was Honor Naval Cadet, commanded the Naval Company as a senior and won the company drill competition, while on the academic side, my top grades earned me membership in the National Honor

Society. That says a lot for receiving the right impetus to inspire one youngster to succeed. And, I am forever thankful for that little talk he gave me. In a small way, I repaid him by painting a portrait of him—and his wife—for the school, which, incredibly, it had never commissioned one to be done while they were alive. I donated both to the school in 2013.

Our proudest moment: Bolles goes to war with the Nation

Bolles School Eighth-grade Cadet Private

All that Fall of 1941, I was throwing myself wholeheartedly into the regimen of the school and delighting in the military aspect, the drilling, the learning of the manual of arms with the actual, the real (inoperable with firing pins removed) rifles—and naïvely taking to it like all the heroes I had read about—and that I fancied being one myself some day. By December, the Battalion of cadets was ready for its first full, dress parade on the football field. All parents would attend, of course, as would the public.

Hardly able to contain my excitement, I couldn't wait until after Sunday dinner to get into my other uniform, the formal "Dress," one: the black long trousers and military 'tunic' with the four patch pockets, the three gold buttons, and the wide black leather belt with the big gold buckle, the lapels, the white shirt and black tie, and this time a 'barracks' hat with black visor and large, round top. Boy, I was fit to spit! And, my parents stood by admiringly before we drove to the school.

Before the parade on that day, the 7th of December, 1941, a lot of cadets and their families assembled in the big visiting room in the main building for a band concert. The school band played a couple of rousing pieces, then in the middle of one, the Faculty Commandant of Cadets, Major Hooker, came bursting in, interrupting the concert and with trembling voice announced that the Japanese had just attacked the United States in Hawaii! **We were now at war!**

Everyone gasped and I don't recall whether the concert continued. But, when all of us three hundred cadets assembled in our platoons and companies on the parade field, we had real reason to strut proudly. We were part of a para-military that would aid the war effort—there was no doubt of that. And, many of us would graduate and enter it. My little chest just about burst the three gold buttons off my tunic...as I marched to the beat of the drum and passed-in-review of the reviewing stand with the Headmaster and the faculty all dressed in their Army uniforms. When the Star-Spangled Banner played, we all—I'm sure—were swelling with patriotism.

After the parade that was all anyone could talk about. And, the newspapers and radio were full of the news of Pearl Harbor. Hardly anyone, though, knew where Pearl Harbor was or why it was attacked—except little lo' me; I had read a big article about Pearl Harbor that previous spring in *Colliers* or *Saturday Evening Post* all about our Naval base there and the ships and how impregnable it was.

The next day, the Headmaster halted all classes so everyone at school could listen to the historic radio broadcast of President Roosevelt and hear him exhort those famous words: "December the 7th...A Day of infamy...and that a 'State of War' now existed between the United States and the Empire of Japan..." Who of us who heard those immortal words spoken by the president could every forget them? Two days later, we heard that Germany and Italy had also declared war on the United States. I remember all too vividly a poster that was soon put up in the dining hall that showed a menacing Nazi soldier with bayonet-mounted rifle and the words underneath: "𝕳eute 𝕰s gibt 𝕯eutschland—𝔐organ die ganz 𝔚elt!" (Today Germany—Tomorrow the whole world!).

So, now the United States was in the big war against half of the world.

My sister and I at River Road in 1942.

139

Chapter 12

Life on River Road—and the river

Those eight and ninth grade years I spent at my grandparents' new house were blissful. My room was on a back corner overlooking the goldfish pond and garden. It wasn't all that conducive to making model airplanes, although I did make a few solid balsa ones of Pan American Clippers that were top attractions at the time, advertising romantic routes across the Atlantic and the Pacific (On my way to the Korean war ten years later, I also flew the Pacific in a military version of one, stopping en route on the tiny atoll of Wake Island that had been an overnight stop for the Pan American Pacific Clippers and where that heroic stand of the Marines took place right after Pearl Harbor). Besides, after a full day at Bolles, followed by dinner, there was only time for homework before going to bed. I'd usually get up in the morning when I heard my grandfather, Daddy Avery, go downstairs and out the front door to pick up the morning paper. I would do my ablutions then see how many push-ups I could do before dressing in my uniform. I got up to 50—but, then, I only weighed about 100 pounds. I only got my weight up to 125 when I reached senior year.

Saturdays and Sundays were free, of course, so I was could roam the neighborhood on my bicycle, go to a friend's house, or whatever.

The river out front always beckoned, too. It was the widest part where it flowed up from the south and made its turn into the narrow channel traversing the city and all the way twenty winding miles to empty into the Atlantic Ocean. At its mouth there, lines of huge granite rocks extended a couple of hundred yards out on each side restricting the ingress and egress and preventing sediment from infiltrating the beaches. They were called "Jetties" and had been laid around the beginning of the century. They were an attraction, too, for climbers—many of whom injured themselves—so caution signs were spotted along their lengths. Fishing was very good along them—but no swimming was allowed as the waves splashed forcefully against them constantly.

It is claimed that the St. Johns River is only one of two in the world that flow north; it and the Nile (the Rhine? Marne?). It originates in a wide basin a hundred miles to the south around Sanford, Florida, in the orange grove region. Not always realized is the fact that Florida rests on top of a large system of underground rivers and lakes due to its limestone base, which accounts for its numerous and sudden sink holes that sometimes take down with them roadways and even houses. Like all southern rivers, the St. Johns has its share of wildlife: alligators and water moccasins or other water snakes, and under the surface an abundance of fish, especially the both abhorred and tasty catfish. What unwary fishermen sometime fail to realize in time is that the catfish has a razor-sharp dorsal fin that can inflict a nasty gash. Crabbing and shrimping are (were) also very productive efforts. Recreationally, the entire river is so wide that boating activities are constant, especially sailboating.

A wide cement bulkhead runs along the river bank from the downtown bridges all the way out near Bolles school, as it did on the other side of the river near Lomax street, far to the south bank down past Ortega. Just beyond Ortega and the Florida Yacht and Timmuquana country clubs was the now enormous Naval Air Station —in fact, this naval facility was directly across from the school. It was fascinating to see the river being used for aircraft training: first, there were the two-place mono-seaplanes perched on top of a single, long pontoon and balanced by a much smaller one at each wingtip to keep them from entering the water. They were known as "Kingfishers," built by Vought-Sikorsky aircraft and were used for training and for observation when assigned to and hoisted aboard battleships and cruisers.

The other observation type plane which was much more prevalent were the Consolidated PBY flying boats that seemed to be constantly landing and taking off on the river. It was a beautiful airplane: it had the boat-type hull of an amphibian and a wide center post on top of which was the broad wing sprouting two engines (propeller types). Its tail section was also raised to avoid water spume as well as take advantage of the airflow from the two elevated engines. On each side between the wing and tail was a plexiglass "blister" turret for the waist gunners. Aerodynamically it was perfect and with its long range, it became a workhorse of the Navy during the war.

The vaunted Consolidated PBY "Catalina" patrol aircraft

A neo-Huck Finn?

That first year I lived with my grandparents on the river (1941-42), there was a lot of activity along the bulkhead. At night, fishermen would walk along it in front of all the houses and drop hand-packed balls of meal of some kind into the water, then scrape barnacles off the bulkhead below the water line with a long hoe-shaped tool, then come back a short time later with big flashlights and, as one shined the light on the spot where the meal bait had been tossed, the other would take a good-sized net, put one of the lead sinkers of the bottom rope between

142

his teeth, with the other hand swing the round net so it opened fully in the air before plopping down into the water where the lighted spot was...letting it sink into the shallow water...then slowly pulling the center rope that went through a collar to contract the net...and then haul it up and reopen it on the grass a foot or so from the bulkhead. To our amazement—and delight—a bunch of reddish, squirming, and smelly shrimp and an occasional crab would pile up and be scooped forthwith and dumped into a larger container while the other man cleared the net. Before leaving for the next spot, they would often give the residents in front of whose house it was, a good quart or so of shrimp as a gift. Times were still hard and if these men were not doing this commercially they were doing it to put food on the family table. We had the cook prepare them for us as well.

After a few years, however, this bountiful shrimp harvest disappeared—no more! Everybody came to the same conclusion that it was due to the activity of the Naval Air Station—the constant aircraft and boat noises in the water and oil leakage pollution driving them away.

Our short dock was a real attraction. I and many others tried fishing from it. I simply was not cut out to be a fisherman (thought it awfully boring, for one thing) and I think I only ever caught one fish, a tiny brim, which I disgustedly threw back. The water was always dark and foreboding...with lots of junk floating in it, many of which were puzzling little long white deflated balloons. I think somebody explained what they were (used condoms—which I mispronounced as 'cun-yuns' but wasn't quite sure what they were used for) and cautioned against anyone fetching them out of the water. My little sister wanted me to fetch one for her one day, but I firmly dissuaded her.

She and I did play one game on that dock that didn't turn out so well. I would have her stand out at the end and I would see if I could walk out to her with my eyes closed—and she guiding me by saying, "go left or go right." Well, we did that a couple of times and I think she tried it, too. But the last time I did it—and I mean the very last time I ever did it—she said right and I went left—right over the edge of the dock and—*splash*—right into the murky water! Bobbing to the surface and spiting out a filthy mouthful, all I could think of was those catfish with their razor-sharp dorsal fins—or those water moccasins we spotted swimming around all the time. I swam as fast as I could around to the other side and climbed up on the lower boat deck and sprawled out to catch my breath. So ended that little game as far as I was concerned.

With all that water and my interest in things naval, I wanted a boat badly. Mr Saxby next door got word of that and he had one on his dock next to ours that he never used; so, he up and gave it to me—to my sheer delight. He helped me float it over to our dock and haul it up onto the lower deck, then I went to a boat store and got two cans of different shades of dark and light blue marine paint.

Laboriously over the next several weekends I sanded and prepared the boat while it rested upside down on that lower level. When I deemed it ready, I painted it lovingly, allowing each layer to dry properly and when all finished, I gingerly launched it into the water. It was a little skiff so built for an outboard motor, not oars. Somehow I manager to propel it, probably with a paddle. And—*voilá*—I was captain of my ship. Despite this non-conforming example of seamanship, I did paddle around never straying far from the dock, except one time when I cruised around and under the nearby high-arched bridge a block from the house that the teens named, "The Thrill Bridge," since they got such a thrill hitting it by their speeding-up their cars and flying a foot or two off in the air before landing on the other side—thankfully never into an on-coming car.

Under that bridge, in a dark area between it and the bulkhead, as I passed, a negro woman stood up bare-breasted and quickly put her blouse back on as a negro man got up and the two high-tailed it up onto the street. A bit taken aback—figuring they had been doing something naughty—I paddled on into the small lagoon that was called Lake Marco and otherwise enjoyed the voyage. Back in those days female anatomy was suppressed in visual representations—never any pictures of even brasiers, except in Sears & Roebuck catalogues; I knew what they covered because I had sneaked a peek at a neighbor one time when she was unaware of me. But that was all; my youthful libido was just forming.

144

Hurricanes?—So what!

Storms in north Florida went with the territory; there were invigorating "Nor'-Easters" that were especially awesome at the beach and daily thunder showers that drove the thermometer down from 98 to 95 or so. But occasionally—and I don't remember anyone particularly referring to a recurring time each year for hurricanes—although one or two that I distinctly recall came through. But we never really expected them late each Summer and early Fall. They were always a surprise.

Back then there was no plethora of meteorologists as there is today; certainly no accurate prognostications of what might portend. Even throughout World War II, predicting weather was iffy, mostly trying to compile weather reports from distant points and then interpolating them into a "probability estimate." That must have been what happened, probably around 1943 just after I had finished painting my new boat. A hurricane was predicted to hit Jacksonville shortly around a certain time in mid-day on a certain date (I guess from reports from the Caribbean or Bahamas). Anyway, it was announced on radio so we all took the only precautions we knew how to: close the windows, get some extra water and wait it out. In previous ones, we had been at the beach house and actually went surfing with our proto-surf boards, three short cypress boards nailed together and the front rounded off. We'd place them against our waists and then try to hop a wave and float with it all the way until we ran aground. During a hurricane was the best time because all the wind and waves were coming in toward shore and would bring us in with them. No one ever got hurt and we didn't ever give that a thought.

So when this big one was predicted for Jacksonville, we took it in stride. I, however, lashed my new boat upside down on the lower dock —the bottom of the hull up to deflect the rain.

The winds ripped in howling and the water churned and the waves whipped and the clouds blocked out the sun and we were hurricane struck. After several hours—toward late afternoon—it abruptly ended.

The wind and rain stopped, the sun came back out and the fleecy clouds heralded rejuvenation. We all relaxed and ventured outdoors. I checked my boat; the high tide was lapping at its sides but it was still tightly bound. I decided since the storm was over I would leave it like that until the tide receded. So everybody went about their usual business—

—until an hour later—when **Wham!**—the storm returned with a vengeance! Worse than the earlier one (we thought this was a second one), higher winds, more violent and destructive. Trees started toppling, water from the river splashed all the way up to our front porch. We had the front floodlights turned on (the electricity must not have gone out yet) and in the growing darkness of evening we watched helplessly as the enormous waves of the angry river swelled, coming right toward us, lifting the boards off the dock in their undulating repetition as they did so...wave after wave for hours, it seemed...until the boards started really breaking away and flying off in the ferocious wind and darkness. We all watched stunned as the large end of the dock heaved and began to come apart, too. The surging waves caught it up like a spatula lifting a fried egg and tossed it into the black nothingness. Gone! The entire dock—that beautiful little dock we loved so much—gone! And—my precious boat with it. All disappeared in the raging torrent and surging surf. And with them—my visions of a life on the river akin to Huck Finn's.

Everyone was puzzled about the two storms. How in the world...? Slowly the information seeped to us that we had been in the "eye" of the storm as it passed over the city. So little was known of hurricanes back then, it took a lot of explaining in the newspapers and on radio just what that "eye" had been. Wouldn't one have imagined that with a previous 500-year history of exploration in 'these here parts' that someone would have put together the fact that a hurricane being a cyclonic storm had a clear center in it? At least have experienced it like Jacksonville did? Maybe that was known but it sure surprised us.

The next day (school classes were called off), I trudged all along the bulkhead in front of all the houses with the debris-strewn lawns down toward the south looking for my boat among the flotsam bobbing up and down in the still not calm water. Way, way, down, near the end of

River Road I found it—or what was left of it. The top half at the Gunwale and seats had been sliced off as if by a buzz-saw and at the bottom of the hull along the keel line there were jagged gashes. I could not even give it a decent burial at sea; all I could do was return home, very dejected. That ended my only possession of a boat but not my boating days; there were still those in the naval unit at Bolles which I sailed and rowed to my heart's content.

The new bicycle

It was obvious even to my grandparents that at 14 I had outgrown my junior, 20-inch wheel Junior bicycle, and I had been giving strong hints that a new, 26-inch would be great for Santa to bring me for Christmas.

Evidently the prices were marked down or something but about a month before Christmas, Daddy Avery took me to a store to choose one that suited me. Boy!—was that great!

I chose a beautiful tan and gold colored Schwinn with white side-walled balloon tires and simulated 'tank' beneath the top bar as well as a cover over the drive chain. I couldn't wait to ride it...

....except that Daddy Avery said that I could not until Christmas day. So, there stood this marvelous new enticement on its kick stand in front of the fireplace for four long weeks. Often I would just sit astride it and imagine how wonderful it was going to be to ride it.

When Christmas day arrived—I was out at dawn riding around the neighborhood. I prized that bike and kept it spotless...shining it all the time and even tying a thin leather thong around each axel so grit and grease would not build up. In my senior year, when such juvenile things had passed, it was still in mint condition and I was very pleased to sell it to a mother who could not afford the retail price for a new one for her son. I think I asked $10.

Puppy love

Back in those innocent pre-teen years no one knew specifically about the "birds and the bees." There was natural speculation but no factual instruction, either from parents (at least not mine) or schools; nor was it garnered from books, magazines, or movies. When the actors kissed and the scene faded, we always suspected there was more to it than we were shown. The movie censor, the Hayes Committee, would not even allow married couples (in the storyline) to be shown in bed together—there always had to be twin beds in the room (never mind that my parents and grandparents slept in separate beds). Some women wore two-piece bathing suits exposing their mid-drifts but the Bikini had not been created yet (except by the Romans two thousand years prior as discovered in murals unearthed in the ancient city of Pompeii that was buried under volcanic ash when nearby Mount Vesuvius erupted).

So there we were, a group of pre-teens wondering some times and the one braggart telling all sorts of inexplicable things to the others. I had been smitten with Frances Cohen back in Tampa...and maybe Mary DuPree...and...

...Well, the spell was broken when Bolles buddy Hugh Powell invited me to a party at his house. I must have been going on fourteen. He said there would be both boys and girls so I was a little apprehensive, since I was a bit shy. It turned out to be fun and the refreshments were enjoyed, then came time for the games: someone suggested "Spin the Bottle" (Hugh, of course). So, a milk bottle appeared out of nowhere and we all gathered in a circle. The one whose turn it was to spin the bottle would be the one kissed by the person the small end of the bottle ended up pointing at (spun again if it landed on the same gender). Well, my turn came and rather timidly (I did not personally know everyone there) I got out in the middle and spun the bottle on the floor...it stopped pointing at a girl! A girl I did not know...but she looked nice, a tiny bit taller that I was.

So, off we scurried to the other room...whereupon she turned and kissed me smack on the lips! Hers were soft and luscious...and I trembled all over—and *it* was over in two seconds—but *I* wasn't. I just stood there as she turned and went back to the other room. I stood mesmerized...my head swirled...I felt I was in a cloud...I couldn't get my mind off those luscious lips of hers—and the fact that I had actually kissed a girl—in the real way, like in the movies, and I felt like I *was* in the movies. In a daze, I joined the others. I didn't play again but just hung in the background relishing what had just happened to me. The girl I had kissed—or had kissed me—was still playing another round and enjoying another disappearance to the other room.

I guess my folks picked me up afterwards—I don't remember—or cared. I was floating off somewhere else.

And that feeling lasted the entire weekend. My grandfather asked me what was wrong with me and I had to come out of it for a few seconds to assure him I was OK...then back to my reverie—that I have cherished, Lo, these many years. I wonder what her name was? And, I guess the kiss didn't affect her like it did me.

As life will have it, I enjoyed many, many more throughout my lifetime.

As my libido was awakened, I began to notice girls more, and joyfully the Bolles School held periodic dances to which cadets brought dates. I don't recall the girls I dated first—of course driven to and from by my parents, usually stopping by a florist first to buy a $5 corsage. My parents had insisted I join a Cotillion that gave ballroom dancing lessons on Saturday mornings. There, we HAD to dance because our parents had paid for our instruction in foxtrot, waltz, rumba, and a fast thing that we could dance to "In the Mood."

I don't quite remember how I met her—it could have been when riding my bicycle over in a residential section adjacent to ours—but Bertie Seewald came into my heretofore one-track life. She was beautiful. Rather tall—I guess as tall as I was. She had beautiful blond hair and a smile that charmed me almost as much as our first kiss in her living room while her mother   was out shopping or something. Just as infatuations go, we talked incessantly. Laughed about everything, reveled in each other, wanted to see each other every day—

or at least hang on the telephone for hours it seemed—*my Gosh*—I was in love!—madly! I could't concentrate on anything else but Bertie. I spent more time on the telephone talking nothingnesses every evening than doing my homework. We got to the point of experimental 'necking'—hugging and kissing—but, just like in the movies, that's as far as it got—as if I knew what was next! Back then we only guessed what "petting" and "all-the-way" were but couldn't conceive what it really entailed, despite the dirty talk some of our friend (not Bertie's) were only too free with.

Bertie Seewald: need I point out why I was attracted?

While I thought this love-of-my-life would never end somehow it fizzled out after a year—or maybe it was because I moved to Ortega Terrace across the river in 1944 when my parents moved down from

Atlanta. Or, was it because I met (again how?) Mary Jo Stroud—and what a beauty she was! Totally opposite of Bertie; long black hair and deep blue eyes, rather busty...and just gorgeous. She lived at the south end of River Road and I don't think I rode my bicycle down there to call on her...but as to   dating, I think I could drive the car then, so even though living way, far across the river, I must have still dated her over on the Southside.

Anyway, when I took her to a Bolles school "Ball," she came in a stunning chiffon-flowing long dress and a GWTW "Scarlett O'Hara" wide-brimmed straw hat. All eyes turned to her as she made a breathtaking image strolling along under the Spanish moss-draped pathways on the river front. She was something out of a Renoir.

Mary Jo Stroud

All very chaste—we only necked occasionally.

Commemorative portrait I did in 2013 in honor of
LtCol Roger M. Painter, co-founder in 1933
of The Bolles School

Chapter 13

On Apache Avenue in Ortega Terrace

I must have been in the tenth grade, in 1944, and 15 when I moved from my grandparents on the Southside over across the river to Ortega Terrace, a relatively new neighborhood but beautifully settled with attractive houses, far beyond Lomax Street, out on the outskirts of town near the very active Naval Air Station, since the war had been going on now for two years.

The house was on a large wooded corner lot at the beginning of the "Terrace," and between us and the old part of Ortega was a wonderful forrest that just invited exploration. It was a relatively new house, two stories with attached two-car garage. It was very spacious inside with a stairway right at the front entrance ascending to the upper floor. There were three good-sized bedrooms all opening to the balustraded half-hall that looked down onto the stairway. My room was on the back west corner and it was all paneled in a blond wood with a built-in bookcase and lower cupboards consuming the entire back wall. Perfect for my books, do-dads, odd and ends, books about war planes and ships and stuff, and especially my accumulating collection of comic books—which were mostly about supernatural figures fighting the nasty Nazis. (After college and when I was off in the Korean War, my parents cleared out my—I guess "childish"—things and gave my prized books and the entire comic book collection to a second-hand bookstore. Somebody got rich off those comic books! They were a priceless collection. Fortunately, by a minor miracle I retrieved the autographed book of his life during World War I that Captain Eddy Rickenbacker had given me in the hospital in Atlanta in 1941)

The room was perfect for my building my model airplanes now on a grand scale. (By the time I left for college, I had 100 models strung across the ceiling on strings. I even built a simulated flight trainer that I could sit in like a cockpit and a stick to control the ailerons and tail elevators and rudder. Once a visiting naval officer was invited up to see my "Hangar"—as all visitors were by my proud Dad—and he promptly invited me to come out to the Naval Air Station and 'fly' in a real Link Trainer. I did and added another thrill to my exciting life.)

Building model airplanes consumed a greater part of my free time after school and in the summers when I wasn't playing softball in one of the grassy fields nearby, or bicycling all over the place, or exploring the woods across the road—or taking piano lessons from a family friend. We, of course, had acquired a piano, a spinet that had excellent tone. (In retrospect, I know that this was all underwritten by my grandfather; I sensed Dad didn't make much money and Mother always had everything her heart desired. Even though the Depression of the '30s was over, the ensuing war years still forced restraint. Dad's car was a 1939 Studebaker two-door that cost $600 just before the war. It was stick-shift, light, tinny, and spartan—good for those times with gas rationing; I don't remember what kind Mother had, but of course she had to have her own (Daddy Avery again).

Thirty-six-inch wingspan model I built of an early Curtiss P-40 that I fashioned with a sliding canopy and control stick that moved all the control surfaces

Musical Interlude

As I was writing this, a tune resurrected itself in my mind...**Dah**-tah-**da**-ta—**da**-ta-da... and it took some time for the words to come back: "Put another nickel in, in the nickel-lo-de-an...I just..." and the rest failed me. There were many catchy, comedy tunes during the war: "A Tisket, a tasket, A brown and yellow basket...I took a letter to my mom"...about taking it to your grandmother or something. Another: "Little old lady, dressed in blue"...something about being true. But the jazzy ones were: "Three Little Fishes"—"Up from the river came three iddy-bitty fish, making their way to the big blue sea...Boop, boop, dittum-dottem-wattum-choo...and they swam and they swam right over the dam"...*or some such inanity.* One that swamped the country was: "Mare-z-doats, an' doez-e-dotes, an' liddle-lamz-e-d'eye-vy—a kiddle-e-d'eye-vy too—wooden you?" Everybody was singing this delightedly as Spike Jones and his comedic orchestra was making hilarious fun of Nazi-German dictator, Adolf Hitler, with a smashing, discordant, slap-happy, crashing sound effects-ridden rendition of "Der Fuehrer's Face" and other raucous, rollicking, silly and witty variations on "Cocktails for Two," the "Blue Danube," the "William Tell Overture" and other great musical hits. Another novelty tune that comes to mind was "Pistol-Packin' Mama." One that really caught on was the "Hut-Sut " song: "Hut-sut Raulson on the rillerah and a brawla, brawla, sooit..." Those silly words came back to me but I had to

Google to find out if it was just gibberish—and it was—by a Swedish composer. All the Big Bands and vocalists played it and the public never tired of it—I guess.

The top tunes of the 1930s and '40s have never been equaled—to me, at least. The "Big Band" music during he war was a big morale booster during somber days. They are still feasts for the ears, stirs to the heart, and pleasures to the memory.

Geography lessons

Sixth grade geography in Tampa was a subject I had taken to heartily—thus I knew the basic globe quite well. (I only point this out because when I taught in an exclusive prep school in 1988, some of the 12th grade students could not even find Japan on the map!) Consequently, all during the war, I would ponder the newspaper accounts of battles and where they took place. It was a tangential education that served me well in later careers, one of which was as a military historian.

From Pearl Harbor, Wake Island, through the Doolittle Raid on Tokyo, to the first counter offensive by the U.S. in the war, the Marine landing on Guadalcanal during the first seven months of 1942, I followed the war then through the North African campaign, the Pacific, the Italian, and European campaigns. Had we been tested at Bolles on the Second World War, I would have made high marks. A lot of other kids would have as well, but, whether they kept up this much or not, I knew ever country's fighting aircraft, ships, uniforms, and weaponry. Back then the movies made about the war were, of course, very accurate in details that were current; today, I have fun viewing later war movies and detecting mistakes in many details (I realize, of course, that it is hard to replicate those precise things from almost three quarters of a century ago, but I think the ignorance of younger producers makes for a lot of it. The exceptions are Steven Spielberg's great "Saving Private Ryan" and Clint Eastwood's similarly great, "Flags of Our Fathers" and "Letters from Iwo Jima," which are impeccable.

During World War II, the movie industry shored up patriotism—as if that were needed. The whole country was war-oriented and every man, woman, and child pitched in to help the war effort. The movies showed the glimpses of the agony and brutality of war, but the U.S was always righteous and the victor—which really was not far from the truth. Sometimes we had to fight ruthlessly and viciously, but the U.S. serviceman was not the inhuman butcher that the barbarian "Jap" or the "Nazi" was. And, what the United States did to heal the wounds and destruction following that war was a lesson in humanity to all mankind (some who heeded it and other who did not).

A commissioned work I painted in 1993 for the Marine Corps University at the Quantico, Virginia, Marine Base; a reconstruction of a moment with the command group during the fierce battle for the Pacific island of Guadalcanal in 1942. The central figure, Col Gerald Thomas, was later the commanding general of the 1st Marine Division I in which I served in the Korean War in 1951.

Chapter 14

A kid's dream: a *close* "War" experience

Take a kid—a wild-eyed 14-year old kid—relishing in the quasi-military atmosphere of a military prep school...and he is in the 10th grade with the quasi-Navy rank of Signalman 3rd Class denoted by the real U.S. Navy insignia worn on his left sleeve only, as a 'specialist' rather than 'line' non-commissioned officer—just like in the real Navy—and having actually passed many of the real Navy qualifications for that rank: knowing Morse code, the International Flag Hoists, ship profile identifications, even semaphore signaling, and besides that, he has kept abreast of the ongoing war, especially those naval battles and the horrendous ones that didn't get as much publicity that were in the Battle for the Atlantic, and you've got a ready sponge. All during the war, even before U.S. forces invaded North Africa in the fall of 1943 and then fought their way up the Italian peninsula before the D-Day landing in France on June 6th, 1944, the U.S. shipped continuous multi-hundred freighter convoys of war matériel and humanitarian relief to England and the Soviet Union via the North Atlantic. The Germans, having learned well from their dominance in submarine warfare during the First World War, exceeded that with deadly "Wolf Packs" of submarines that sank Allied shipping all the way from England to the Caribbean—and along the Eastern Seaboard of the United States. German subs launched Nazi saboteurs onto Ponte Vedra beach within several miles of our beach house and often brazenly came to the surface during nighttime to torpedo and shell defenseless American "Liberty Ships" loaded with cargoes heading for Europe within sight of the beaches.

Well...with all the above commonly known, the thrill of a lifetime presents itself to this very receptive boy: the opportunity to go— *actually ride in/on*—a real Liberty Ship that will be sailing down the St. Johns River, through the jetties, and out to sea just off Jacksonville Beach! *Actually go into a war zone!* It's something that requires great effort to avoid peeing in one's pants in excitement.

You can guess who the fortunate boy was; and it came about through a non-Bolles friend of his, whose father ran one of the two ship-building dock-yards on the city waterfront. Ship building in Jacksonville was a big industry during the war, and I think two big Liberty Ships were launched per month—something like that.

As one might imagine..I could hardly contain myself—or my bladder—until the day came.

A typical Liberty Ship that carried war matériel and food in massive convoys across the North Atlantic to relieve England and Russia. Of the thousands that made the journeys, some 3,000 were torpedoed by German "Wolf Pack" submarines with great loss of life.

Reporting aboard, Sir!

Attired in my Bolles cadet uniform—*what else?*—with my Signalman's chevron, I was deposited at the ship yard at 3:00 AM by my sleepy-eyed Dad. There, my friend and his father and a crewman met me and we all boarded the giant vessel.

My wild eyes could not believe it! On a real Navy ship—but it wasn't exactly Navy, it was manned by the Merchant Marine; only the gun crews were U.S. Navy. *Gun crews*! Real guns—cannons—right there where I could touch them...and their crews in their Navy fatigue uniforms. When they saw me, they smiled and gave me a salute—to which I returned a very snappy one.

My friend, Ken Merrill, and I were free to explore the entire ship so long as we stayed away from operating machinery and crew drills and such. Now that I think about it, we were not even issued life vests...it was assumed we had sense enough not to fall overboard (what if we were torpedoed?). The slow twenty-mile passage up the river to the ocean took us straight into the rising sun and the marvelous coloration of the clouds and water. My grandfather had taken me when I was about four on a passenger steamship of the Merchants & Miners Steamship Line out of Jacksonville to Savannah, for which he had worked before he acquired the Union Terminal Warehouse company; but of that voyage, I only remembered the scary elevated walkway through a large building and then the railings on shipboard...beyond that, memories fade.

Being a Navy signalman myself, I naturally sought out the ship's signalman. I don't know whether he was Navy or Merchant Seaman, but he took me under his wing...and upon discovering that I, indeed, did know a lot about signaling, he let me signal in morse code with the spotlight that had a shutter over the lens and a handle in order to open the light for a short burst or a long burst, indicating the dots and dashes of the code. There was no recipient ship, of course, but it was a thrill upon a thrill. When we stood nearby when the Navy crews practice fired the 40-mm cannon at the stern and the 50-calibre anti-aircraft machine guns—I was enthralled! Real guns firing on a real ship in a real war zone. WOW! Would that be a story when I got back to Bolles in the Fall.

> **Historical note:** The Merrill-Stevens shipyard (of the St. Johns River Shipbuilding Company) only operated a little over three years during the war. Employing 20,000 workers, it turned out 82 ships. Liberty ships displaced 14,400-tons of water, cost two million dollars apiece and could travel 10,000 miles at 11 knots (13 miles per hour). They sailed in 200-500-ship convoys, only protected occasionally by a U.S. Coast Guard cutter and spaced out over dozens of square miles of sea, and zig-zagging on courses to try to avoid or make it harder for the lurking German submarines to track and torpedo them. As it was, out of the thousands of ships and hundreds of convoys that brought cargo and munitions to both England and the Soviets (via their ice-free port at Murmansk in the Arctic Circle), almost three thousand of these vessels were sunk en route. More were sunk in the Caribbean, off the Florida and New England coasts, and clustered off the Sierra Leone African, English, and Spanish coasts than near England or Russia. By the end of the war the Germans had also lost their entire fleet of more than 300 U-Boats, sunk by Allied naval ships and aircraft. These were in the days before Radar and Sonar and locating them was by visual observation.
>
> The unsung heroes of World War II were certainly the Merchant Seamen who, although not combatants, unflinchingly gave their all in high-risk at sea and more often than not, in combat—or suffered as a result of combat.

An actual event experienced by noted Maritime artist, Anton Otto Fischer, then a Coast Guard officer whose specific duties were to paint pictures of the sea warfare in the North Atlantic. (From my book, Art of War, 2002)

Another adventure at sea

So, not content with simply having "gone down to the sea in ships"—
A Liberty ship—I now had an opportunity to go out to sea—*solo—in my
own ship...boat—OK, raft*. It was my sixteenth birthday in mid summer
before I entered 11th grade and we were staying down at the beach
house. Somehow my parents were able to buy—probably from a
military surplus store—a one-man, yellow, inflatable rubber life raft for
my gift..which, within minutes I had down at the edge of the surf and
was releasing the compressed air bottle letting the little thing pop into
life. It was the type used in aircraft for pilots having to ditch into the
water. There were two short aluminum oars and a raised hard rubber
grommet on each side for them to mount through. Other than that, all
you had to do was sit yourself in it and row away—which I commenced
to do right away—headed for Africa!

*My own new sea-worthy vessel in which I embarked eastward
toward the open sea on my sixteenth birthday.*

I bobbed through the surf and tumbled into it in my wet bathing
trunks and began rowing eastward. I looked back toward the beach but

nobody had come to see me launch...just as well; there would have been lots of admonitions.

So, here I was at sea again in those very same waters that the German U-boats and the Liberty ships had sailed, only I wasn't quite that far out—*yet*!

The Atlantic was calm and I did not spot any ominous fins coming toward me nor any friendly porpoises surfacing and blowing water spumes...so on I rowed.

An hour passed perhaps and the water began to get a bit choppy and I turned to look back—and the shoreline with the row of beach houses was far, far off on the horizon, barely discernible (of course, my viewpoint was right there at water level, so that made a difference). It was then that a gleam of better judgment got to me...and I turned around and headed back to shore.

The wind had changed direction to off-shore and I was now heading into it, which made for slow progress. There were no small boats or even shrimp trawlers to be seen as there usually were. I was all alone...just "the *young* man and the sea." I wasn't particularly concerned; I was a good swimmer and it never occurred to me that a shark fin could have deflated the raft in a flash—and then what would I do? I didn't have a life jacket on either.

I rowed and rowed and, of course, my back was toward shore so I could not see where I was heading...every now and then I would have to do a one-eighty to check that I wasn't going around in a circle. When I got somewhat closer and the houses loomed larger, I saw that there was a bunch of people grouped on the beach to which I was aiming—and a vehicle. I wondered what that was all about?

As I finally reached the waves and the surf—which gave me quite a nice finale—drifting in with a wave until the raft beached itself. I got out and turned to see my Mother and the Lifeguard Rescue Team with their own raft and life preservers at the "ready"...just waiting for me to alight. Which I did with a cheerful greeting and asking where the action was?

My Mother lit into me, chastising me for doing such a dangerous stunt. I protested that I didn't see anything wrong—I was in a safe life raft and I could swim.

The gratitude that I had come safely home outweighed the deed, so all ended well. Funny, I never went out in that raft again; I guess that one incident was all I needed to get something out of my system. The anticipated thrill was satiated—or the consequences dawned on me later.

Vivid depictions of the war

In those simpler days less than a decade from the burgeoning television onslaught to come, the newspapers, magazines, and movie newsreels   presented photos and clips from the battlefields as quickly as they could be shipped back via courier airplane.   Telecommunication was in its infancy and a telephone under-sea cable had only connected the U.S. with London fifteen years earlier. So, the most immediate war reports came via radio feeds, mainly from London. The print media was by necessity weeks behind events.

A unique medium became highly developed during the war: visual reports in the form of art—sketches and paintings—from some of America's most distinguished artists of the period. The same had been done in the First World War, only on a smaller scale. Some artists were already serving in the armed forces—and in battle, where they made sketches afterward. In a brilliant stroke, the supreme commander, General Dwight Eisenhower, ordered that the history of the war was to be properly covered by word, photography, and by art. He called upon the army to institute a program for artists discovered already serving in the ranks. The Navy, Marine Corps, and Coast Guard did similarly. The U.S. War Department (after the war to be renamed the "Defense Department") called upon civilian artists to join the government's paid program to send them to war zones to depict what they saw and experienced in their own, uncensored styles. Many big corporations like Abbott Laboratories and magazine publishers like *Life* and *Colliers* did likewise and the collections after the war amounted to over ten thousand works, all now housed in the separate service archives and exhibited from time to time (all in public domain so available for anyone's use).

(The reason I point this out is that in two later wars—after my combat in the Korean War—I, too, became a Combat Artist for the Marine Corps and wrote a seminal book about it: Art of War: Eyewitness U.S. Combat Art from the Revolution through the 20th Century. Barnes & Noble 2002. *More than a hundred of my sketches and paintings are in the Combat Art collection of the National Museum of the Marine Corps at Quantico, Virginia.)*

What leads me to write about this is a 1944 issue of *Life* magazine that I opened and it had the work of a noted Texas civilian artist by the name of Tom Lea. As I turned the pages of his paintings, one almost bolted me out of my chair! It was of a Marine being so badly wounded on the beach at Peleliu that half of his skin was ripped off. Lea had been next to him on the beachhead when he was struck and later portrayed him at the second before he collapsed in an agonizing death.

It was so shocking that the image remained with me for the rest of my life.

A half century later, when I was writing the aforementioned book, *Art of War*, I had the opportunity to meet Tom Lea and take a photo of him standing beside that incredible painting:

Noted American artist, Tom Lea, of El Paso, Texas, a civilian artist hired by Life *magazine to depict battles in WW II, beside his painting, "The Price, " a dying Marine as he was fatally wounded right next to Lea as he accompanied the first wave to hit the beach in the invasion of Peleliu.*

Doing our part for the war

My grandfather, being a businessman in the logistic-supply field, served on various local wartime boards like the port authority, and my father, too old (40s) for active military service, volunteered for the Auxiliary Coast Guard and donned a uniform and sidearm and patrolled the city docks several nights a week. My mother and grandmother did all those things the women were doing like rolling bandages for the Red Cross and collecting Bundles for Britain and for Russia. We kids snooped all over and collected tinfoil from discarded gum wrappers, cigarette packages, and other cast off items and rubber bands, likewise, and rolled them up into larger than softball sizes to turn in for recycling.

Every Sunday, when I was with my grandparents and we attended the Church of the Good Shepherd on Park Street in Avondale, we'd invite a sailor or soldier or two to come back home with us to enjoy a family home-cooked Sunday dinner. After a pleasant time chatting afterward, we would usually drive them downtown to join their buddies at the movies. I would, of course, be dressed in my own Bolles cadet uniform and would thrill associating with *real* fighting men.

Later, my parents rented out my sister's adjoining bedroom (with shared bathroom) to a Navy couple (just married) who preferred to live off base while he underwent advanced flight training at the Air Station. They stayed several months until he was ordered overseas.

At Bolles we would often have a naval officer come over—via the "Captain's Gig (boat)" to give us a talk about the Navy or the war—all very exciting. And, too, several of the faculty members were called up for active duty and so new teachers (no doubt "4-Fs" who failed to be physically fit for military duty and so were grabbed up by schools like Bolles to fill in) appeared to teach and coach. For our part, that is, the Corps of Cadets, we proudly participated in civic parades in downtown Jacksonville, where there were all sorts of patriotic displays, mostly exhibits with actual aircraft and guns from the Naval Air Station. Overhead we constantly saw the Navy's bi-wing trainer, the "Yellow

Peril" (which I got to fly in after the war) and the ubiquitous advanced trainer, the "SNJ" and occasionally the twin-engined Lockheed "Hudson" that had been converted on the production line from the civilian "Electra" version. Army Air Corps planes would fly over, too, and over the war years there were a few mishaps: planes crashing into neighborhoods with loss of life.

Those sad departures for war duty were sentimentalized by the songs of the time: "Don't sit under the apple tree...with anyone else but me" and "When Johnny Comes Marching Home Again..." the Civil War song rearranged by Morton Gould, "Off We Go into the Wild Blue Yonder," "Coming in on a Wing and a Prayer," "Lily Marlene" the German song that hit the short-wave hit parade, the Australian ditty "Waltzing Matilda" and others picked up by our servicemen overseas. Tender love songs like "At Last...my love has come along," could bring a tear.

Most of the Country's leading movie stars, singers, and entertainers volunteered for the USO (United Service Organization) shows that went into the war theaters (battle areas) to entertain the troops: Bob Hope with Frances Langford and troupe, Bing Crosby, *et al.* Popular crooner Dick Haymes opted out of service claiming Argentine citizenship. Other celebrities joined the military and many saw intense combat: actor Jimmy Stewart flew B-17 bombers, Tyrone Power became a Marine aviator, Eddie Albert was in many Pacific battles; many talented soldiers, sailors, and Marines became actors, musicians, even clothes designers (Bill Blass) after the war.

The cultural scene in the U.S. was virtually curtailed save for the likes of the great Broadway show producers like Rogers and Hammerstein, whose "Oklahoma" lifted the spirits of the nation and still is performed today, and Leonard Bernstein's (who avoided military service) "West-Side Story" that still draws crowds as well. The young phenomenon, Frank Sinatra, descended on the scene on the heels of Bing Crosby, Tony Bennet, and Vic Damone. Skinny, young, and attractive with his pompadour-combed hair and mesmerizing baritone, 'Frankie' drew screaming and waving and swooning female teeny-boppers to him by the droves—more than bees to honey. Some of the female greats were Jo Stafford, Dinah Shore, Ginger Rogers, Frances Langford, and Ella Fitzgerald.

Gasoline was rationed to three gallons per week aa well as meat, a lot of appliance and other manufacturing—like automobiles, washing machines (who could afford them anyway?)—were discontinued; toys and anything that used materials that were needed for war vehicles and munitions were turned into making guns, airplanes, and ammunition. Why butter was one of these beats me, but instead of it my mother would buy margarine: a big white chunk of it with a little packet of yellow coloring that came with it. Then she would have to mash that white chunk and mix the coloring into it until it became the color of butter—only taste would tell. I have no idea what that white stuff was…possibly a grease of some kind or perhaps (as I found out later) a lump of lard like the base of peanut butter. Anyway, no one my age seemed to mind or miss the taste of real butter.

Another minor sacrifice to men's fashion was that manufacturers no longer put cuffs on men's trousers, or, I think, made double-breasted suits—that must have saved tons of money and cloth! Saddle oxford shoes were still available as well as the 'Bobby Socks' that went with them. Men still went about clean shaven; only once in a while could the once fashionable pencil-thin mustache—worn by actors like Errol Flynn, Adolph Menjou, and William Powell be seen.

One thing that was quite obvious was that no one was fat. Even in the preceding decade which was, of course, spartan, obesity was a rarity. With a reduced wartime diet a natural slenderness prevailed. "Fast Food" restaurants were not to be invented until long after the war. The only quick service one that was not a typical Diner was a "Toddle House," which was attractively designed and served a limited menu. They still exist.

The Home Front thus was immersed in all things military, as would be expected in this all-out 'World" war. And, I did my part—as long as it didn't take me away from my own interests.

Chapter 15

Carefree youthful times

A pubescent's scourge: Acne

While this ubiquitous affliction can be cured today, back in the 1930s and '40s that was no so. Fortunately, my face only broke out with a few patches on my chin and lower jaw. But it must have reached a stage that my Mother thought something had to be done about it. So she took me to a doctor downtown who, I guess either advertised, or a friend had advised, had a new treatment for the problem.

His treatment—mind you—was to inject 'peanut oil' intra-venously into the bloodstream. When he did that to me, I could feel the warmth of the oil flowing into all parts of my body. Even though I was 14 or so, it occurred to me that since acne was caused (people had said) by oily skin forming pus modules in hair follicles, why in the world would the doctor shoot me with more oil? I had three of these treatments—all to no avail. The only thing that came of them was that the doctor recommended that I drink my coffee black—no cream. I have done so ever since.

I smelled like a peanut candy bar for a week.

My own solution thenceforth was to take a washcloth and run it under the hottest water the faucet would produce, then apply that to the affected area...hold it as long as I could stand it, until the pus head would pop—then I would douse it with rubbing alcohol. That cleared them up right away and I was not left with any scars. Wonder why the doc couldn't figure that out?

I even did this whenever a pesky pimple would arise all the way up into my 40s. I was cautioned not to do this as the pimples were little staph infections and any disturbance like I was doing around the nose area could result in a serious brain infection. I guess vanity beat sanity.

Summer jobs (Halcyon days of youth)

Not that I particularly needed to work in the summertime but I guess the work ethic was instilled in me by the example of my grandfather and dad—or it was to make a bit more than my weekly twenty-five cent allowance.

The first job was as a day counselor at the Good Shepherd's summer day camp for boys. I was 14 or 15. A busload of us would be driven over across town to what would have been termed "the other side of the tracks," although it was all white. There, in a church we had access to a swimming pool and we took walks to a nearby park and ate our bagged lunches and played games and stuff and then were bused back to our church, where I was picked up to go home. It was a two-week thing and a fairly good experience with younger brats.

The next job I had was as a stock boy in the Florida Schoolbook Depository in my grandfather's enormous warehouse building in the industrial area on the edge of downtown Jacksonville. I'm sure it was pre-arranged as the owner of the depository was a close friend of my grandfather's (I didn't think of it at the time, but back in those days it would have been far better to have given the job to a really needy young kid—not me).

Anyway, another kid my age and I worked together fetching a certain amount of books from one source and loading them to be shipped out at another spot. We earned "Minimum Wage" which had come into effect at the time for a grand sum of forty cents (40¢) per hour. (the WPA paid artists $41.25 a month wages; yearly incomes barely exceeded $1,000; the CCC men earned $30 a month (food included), and Army base pay was $20 per month (with free food, clothing, and shelter), and Bolles School tuition was $300 for day-boy and $600 for a border [$20,000 in 2014]). We didn't horse around and worked pretty conscientiously, if I do say so myself. There was a peep hole between the men's and the lady's restrooms—but it was placed inconveniently and did not serve us well.

Perhaps it was the following year, I must have been sixteen Ah... sweet "Sixteen" as the author Booth Tarkenton's popular book was titled—and every kid back then was obligated to read it. I did and thought it was the proper way boys and girls interacted (this was before Bertie Seewald!).

I don't know whether the law had anything to do with working before age sixteen, but the summer I turned that age I did get a great job (again, thanks to family) with a prestigious advertising agency that sent a unit down from Atlanta (Tucker Wayne) to do some filmstrips about nutrition or something. My artistic talent was recognized beyond kid stuff to some pretty good serious things (and I had been studying with artist Harold Hilton—where that tall girl Kitty was). So—mind you —I joined that professional adult group and became the "story board" artist on the project, that is, I would sketch the fruit and vegetables and words onto each successive little picture box in the series of a dozen or so (what are now termed "Power-Point Presentations") and a professional artist in Atlanta would use those to do the finished art. That was an incredible credit for my later résumés and one of the jobs I had later on Madison Avenue in New York city was just that: as an art director doing story boards for national television commercials.

These jobs must have been for a limited time, I don't remember. I know it—nothing—interfered with the time spent at the beach house and all the wonderful activities at the Ponte Vedra Country Club's swimming pool—or at the pool at the Florida Yacht Club out Ortega way. Those were exciting, fun-filled, halcyon days of youth, indeed.

A lapse of sanity

In Ortega Terrace, down the street, a playmate named Paul Traver and I became good friends, we were about 15 at the time. His parents had a cabin way down in the woods in central Florida where they went on short vacations. Paul invited me one time and off we went with his parents. The cabin was off a dirt road a good way into the woods; great for exploring and stuff. Adjacent, oddly, was an Army Air Force airfield. Interesting, though, the airplanes being flown there were Bell P-39 Airacobras, I knew right off because I had made a model of one, so it was fun to watch them. They were unique in that the Allison engine was behind the pilot's cockpit, and forward of it, was a 20-mm cannon mounted internally with the muzzle coming right out of the middle of the propeller cone. I learned later that they were only used infrequently, once at Guadalcanal, and later many were given to the Russians who used them quite effectively against German tanks.

But, we two adventurers did something that thinking upon it afterwards was about the craziest thing anyone could in his right mind do: we would run barefooted through the woods...over twigs and branches...over tree trunks...over underbrush covered with dead leaves...and, when we would come to a pond (usually stagnant, ugly, and dark), we'd venture to wade in it—not giving a thought—not that we had any thoughts in our empty heads—to the snakes and alligators that no doubt lurked there just waiting for something to catch and eat. Luck was with us, for nothing untoward ever happened—even when we jumped over a log—and almost landed on a sunning coachwhip snake! Florida is notorious for its four very poisonous snakes: the water moccasin, the rattlesnake, the copperhead, and, little known, the coral snake. Take it from me: I have spotted all of them in the wild—and many an alligator—from a distance. To this day, I shudder to think about our running stupidly in those woods.

Since then I have learned what every Southern country boy knows before his A-B-Cs: never step over a log, but step up on it and look down on the other side before continuing because most likely that's where an ol' rattler is bound to be lurking.

More halcyon days of youth

At around age thirteen, I learned to drive a car. Dad's 1938-or '39 Studebaker, as mentioned before, was as simple and spartan as necessary for basic transportation (my more well-to-do grandparents always had big Chryslers and Packards). But the Studebaker was OK and easy to drive. It was stick shift in four gears but I caught on to that right away—no problem. There must not have been a student or training license back then or I just don't remember. But, one day, when I must have been in the tenth grade, I had to go to Bolles on a Saturday, and, instead of my Dad having to waste his day taking me and waiting to bring me home, he let me drive myself! (I don't recall Mother's reaction). So, off I went just like a grown up, although I had to strain a bit to look over the steering wheel. Nevertheless, I lived up to their trust and went and returned without mishap. From then on, I think I was allowed to use the car for dates. I don't remember what model car Mother had...she was partial to Plymouths, as I recall.

When the war ended and civilian automobile production resumed and the automobile industry got back into forward gear, my grandfather bought one of the first new Chryslers on the market. It had some new do-dads to make it attractive to a re-emerging market. One thing was a marvelous dashboard in a new thing called plastic. It was varicolored with greenish, yellow, and red color swirls all mixing together (when I think about it now it was positively garish). The interior was plush, too, and it was probably "fluid drive," the marvelous innovation introduced just before the war that eliminated stick shifting. (it is called 'automatic' drive today)

The war had ended, of course, in September of 1945 when I had just entered my senior year at Bolles. So, it must have been after graduation that following summer when my grandfather and grandmother drove to Chicago to visit his brother and family, Herbert and Analyle Avery. They took me along. It was a three-day trip to get there back then; all the highways (that were paved) were two-lanes and there were not too many filling stations along the way. The first stopover was in middle Georgia, in Perry, a quaint little village and we stayed at the Perry

Hotel, built before the Civil War. (If anyone then would have predicted that I would retire and spend my final years within three miles of that hotel—I wouldn't have believed it!).

I don't recall the second stop—there were no motels back then. But, I do remember our reaching a beautiful big farm house on the road in Illinois that had a sign out in front announcing "Dinner being served"— and we arrived just at dinner time (mid-day). It was a big old Victorian house (I didn't know what that was, of course, just that it was big and old). We were escorted into a very large dining room where a dozen or so people were seated at a very big table loaded down with food. We took the remaining seats and it seemed just like home. I think there were lots of places like that before restaurants began sprouting up along highway routes—and way before the McDonald era.

The major factor in this very nice family visit with the Chicago relatives was an introduction Uncle Herbert arranged for me to a real art director at a major advertising agency downtown; I think it was Batton, Barton, Durston, and Osborn (BBD&O). The art director was very gracious and showed me illustrations that had been made for upcoming print ads (there was no TV back then). One was a terrific rendition of some horses or something—probably for a cigarette ad.

The art director said that the artist, whom he had hired, was paid $400 for his work (which was a tremendous amount for those days, when average yearly salaries rarely exceeded a thousand or so dollars.

When I ooo'd and ahhh'd, he said that four hundred dollars did sound good...but what the artist would probably do was spend it foolishly—maybe drink it away—and then have to wait a long time for another art assignment.

Knowing that I was an aspiring artist and would understandably side with the artist, he pointed out that the work of the artist was sporadic—he could not count on a steady income—whereas, he—the Art Director— had a steady job and called all the shots and created the ads...hiring all sorts of artists. He told me to consider if that wasn't a whole lot better that the insecure career of an illustrator—and, this was during the time of the "Golden Age" of illustration, as magazines engaged commercial artist-illustrators constantly. There was a lot of work out there for them and the leading ones like Norman Rockwell,

Jon Whitcom, Andrew Wyeth, John Clymer, Harvey Dunn, Hal Foster, Steven Dohanos, Edwin Georgi, Dean Cornwell, Tom Lea, Peter Hurd, and countless others made good livings during that period.

So, that sage advice stuck with me, and since I had opted out of going to the Naval Academy and decided on an art career of some sort, this art director's advice hit the right nerve. (In my later career, I was not only an art director in advertising, but a commercial illustrator, a fine artist, portrait painter, cinematographer, photographer, digital artist, and combat artist—thus fulfilling more than a single role with works in museums, many collections, prizes for a TV Special, TV commercials, and books—all due to my artistic talent. Not bragging—just making the best of what I was born with. Furthermore, the opportunities were limitless from the 1950s through the '90s)

I can attribute somewhat of a beginning of an art career to when I was at the beach house at age 8 or 9. I found some rectangular pieces of wood and drew crayola renditions of dogs on them...which some neighbors bought. Then, when I was in my later teens—still at the beach—I did some pastel portraits of daughters of friends and earned an astounding twenty bucks each. They were good likenesses, too. (In later life I earned as much as $50,000 for a portrait; and many others of mine are in military, government, private, and museum collections here and abroad)

Naturally, at Bolles, and later in college, I was called upon to do illustrations, cartoons, covers, and stories, posters for magazines, sets for stage plays, sketches for yearbooks and such.

Thinking of Bolles reminded me of one of those teachers who truly affect one's life; that was my eleventh grade English teacher, Mr. Houston; "Chief" Houston. He was elderly and white-haired and he was a pleasant task-master. We had to write reports on the books he assigned us to read. One in particular I recall was "Porto Bello Gold," all about pirates, which I didn't mind—what with my experience with Gasparilla in Tampa and the recent movie, "Captain Blood, starring Errol Flynn as a swashbuckling pirate who was perfectly clean-shaven all the time—a far cry from the 2013 portrayal of a slovenly Captain Jack Sparrow by actor Johnny Depp. I never did figure out, though, just where Porto Bello was; I suspected in the Caribbean. I hated the procedure he insisted we use: we had to first simply write down every thought about the book that came to us, then to rearrange them into a logical flow or storyline. It was drudgery and he would stroll up and down between our desks and check us as we did so. If we wrote a superior paper he would not award a numerical grade but draw a little oak leaf in red on it, meaning a "100."

As much as I disliked doing that prep before writing, it was a lesson that has been embedded in me all my life. I added to that a mental "Beginning—Middle—and Ending" and I can confidently meet any problem, write anything, and especially speak extemporaneously. To him, I am eternally indebted.

Two movies that affected me greatly

During the latter part of my senior year, I saw two movies at the great St. Johns Theater in downtown Jacksonville that I can never forget:

I cannot recall the name of the first one but it was in technicolor and was a series of wonderful musical pieces of all genres set in gorgeous tableaux. Although I had heard many operas and individual arias on the radio, I had never actually seen a performance of one. In this film there was an episode that simply lifted me off my seat: it was the most glorious aria ensemble I had ever heard and the staging was so magnificent and rousing that I was absolutely enthralled: it was the "Brindisi," or Drinking Ensemble from the first act of the opera "La Traviata": *"Libiamo, Libiamo, ne' lieti calici...*I learned the libretto to it but it doesn't come to mind as I write, although I can hear the music quite clearly in my mind.

I might have heard the opera on the radio but hearing AND seeing it acted while being sung was just astounding. It rang in my head long afterward—long enough for me to have sought it out on a recording and bought it. That set me determined to see as many operas as I could, which a couple of years later when I attended Princeton I was able to start doing.

The other movie was "Stairway to Heaven" starring David Niven, who as a wounded RAF (Royal Air Force) pilot coming back from a bombing raid in a shrapnel-riddled airplane started quoting a poem of which only these fragments of lines stuck with me: *"...But at my back I hear...Time's wingèd chariot drawing near...and yonder all before us lie...."* I don't know whether Niven mentioned the poet's name or that I asked my English teacher who gave me the answer, but I had never heard such a beautiful love poem like this before, so I learned it and it has been with me throughout my lifetime: (Of course, back then, I wasn't sure what a 'mistress' was.)

To His Coy Mistress

Had we but world enough, and time,
This coyness, Lady, were no crime.
We would sit down and think which way
To walk and pass our day.
Thou by the Indian Ganges' side
Shouldst rubies find:
I by the tide of Humber would complain.
I would love you ten years before the Flood,
And you should, if you please, refuse
Till the conversion of the Jews.
My vegetable love should grow
Vaster than empires, and more slow;
An hundred years should go to praise
Thine eyes and on thy forehead gaze;
Two hundred to adore each breast,
But thirty thousand to the rest;
An age at least to every part,
And the last age should show your heart.
For, Lady you deserve this state,
Nor would I love at lower rate.
  But at my back I always hear
Time's wingèd chariot hurrying near;
And yonder all before us lie
Deserts of vast eternity.
Thy beauty shall be no longer found,
Nor in thy marble vault shall sound
My echoing song:

Then worms shall try that long preserved virginity,
And your quaint honor turn to dust,
And into ashes all my lust;
The grave's a fine and private place,
But none, I think, do there embrace.

Andrew Marvell (c. 1667)

An Aside: Religion

Why a comment on religion? I only bring this topic up because there wasn't any in my up-bringing. We were Episcopalians so we dutifully attended church—which to me was a complete bore. We considered ourselves Good Christians and led a decent life—but no "Jesus-on-the-sleeve" type of proselytizing. My experiences in Sunday School were nondescript. It started way back in Columbia at the Episcopal church next to the state Capitol building. I was five or six. We were given a biblical drawing to color. Mine was a man sitting on a donkey; I forthwith crayoned in the right place his private parts—causing the aghast teacher to whisk it away from me and into the trash. I couldn't figure what I'd done wrong.

Probably the biggest turn-off was in Tampa a year or two later in the Episcopal church on either S. Plant or S. Hyde Park avenues. There, the preacher (priest?) was named Jack Walthour (who moved to Atlanta and we evidently kept in touch there; he turned out to be somewhat famous). But I distinctly recall his coming in to our Sunday School class and trying to get us to memorize the names of the first five books of the Old Testament: Genesis, Exodus, Numbers, Leviticus, and Deuteronomy. I could not pronounce them nor did they make any sense to me—nor did I see any reason to learn these strange words. Looking back on this episode, I wonder why the Episcopal church was so 'out-of-it' when it came to teaching the Bible? I say this because years later, during my male *menopause* around age 50, I got zapped (presumably then by the Holy Spirit) in an Episcopal church in Jacksonville and went through the "Born-Again" experience, out of which I came away with eight years of intense bible study before—well, that's a whole 'nother story...(which I have written as a *roman à clef* and is available on Kindle and Nook: *Faith: Was it Stephen's wife Faith or his spiritual faith that led him to his Fate?*))

In my mid teens I had, of course, been forced to learn the "Catechism," which, again, was a meaningless rite. It was at St. Marks church in Ortega down a few blocks form our house in Ortega Terrace.

Around that time, a Bolles and neighborhood playmate, Jack Fitch, and I attended church (not Sunday School) packing 'heat.' I had my Dad's .25-calibre Colt automatic pistol in my pocket and I think Jack had something similar. Don't ask me why we did this—just for the dare, I suppose. But, since no one knew, what was the point in doing it? I had been taking the gun apart and cleaning it and putting it back together since I was 12 or so, even shooting it occasionally in the woods across the street.

Nothing to do with religion, but one other prank Jack and I pulled off quite successfully was one early evening after dark, we stuffed a pair of his long pants and a shirt with newspapers or something, got an old hat and a pair of shoes, and dragged them out to a ditch right next to Ortega Boulevard near his house. When there was a break in the traffic, we put the dummy together on the side of the road with a foot in the roadway as if just struck by a car and left to die.

Sure enough! A bunch of cars appeared—one spotted the 'body' lying there—and a slight traffic jam ensued. We high-tailed it behind the bushes and watched. When someone poked it and discovered what a trick it was—he wasn't too happy about it. He shouted for all to hear, "You little B%*&+($@...rds!"

We never got the shoes or the clothes back. Didn't care; we'd had our fun. Oh, god—weren't those innocent days compared to today?

A change of objective: college

Only my senior year (1945-46) at Bolles was not under the shadow of war. I had been aiming toward attending the U.S. Naval Academy, but, when the war ended, I opted for an art degree instead—nevertheless joining the Marine Corps Reserve during my freshman year in college at Sewanee, in a reflex of patriotism and my now embedded fascination with the military.

My five years at Bolles were the most formative of my life. They set a purpose, taught me a structure, afforded me the opportunity to develop to my greatest potential, and awakened a self-discipline that had lain semi-dormant. In short, that high school experience far outshone any I would have gotten at one of the public high schools in Jacksonville. For that, I am eternally grateful to my parents and grandparents for having sent me there.

The first four years at Bolles, I had been a 'day boy', taking the bus each day to and from the school; for my senior year (1945-46), I had been allowed to board, which was important since I had become a cadet officer and boarding represented more responsibilities and the full military experience. I was promoted to naval cadet Lieutenant (equivalent to army captain), commanding the naval "C" Company, comprised of three platoons of three squads. I was never a social leader like class or student body president, instead, I went in for artist for the year book, the monthly publication, and some other extraneous groups. I was pint-sized and underweight for my age, only attaining 5-feet six-inches in my senior year. Consequently, I did not go out for football or basketball but did make the swimming team as a diver. During athletic period, I mostly stayed down at the boathouse and did boating, sailing, marlinspike seamanship, and the like.

Funny: another boy and I were the smallest in our class of 1946. Joe Kittinger was in the band and I, in the naval unit; yet, only he and I went into the military after college to the extent of rising to the rank of colonel and being in combat. Kittinger became a noted space pioneer, a fighter pilot and prisoner of war in Vietnam; I joined the Marines and fought in Korea, Vietnam, and the later Gulf War. We both benefitted from our Bolles military training and we still chat at school reunions.

Graduation at Bolles: June 1946

Naval Cadet Lieutenant Chenoweth

When that long-anticipated day arrived, it had culminated in a bevy of customary activities: the parents all gathered, the cadets in their summer dress uniforms with the white trousers, white belts, and white caps, all 52 of us graduating seniors gathered on the river lawn of the campus for the plethora of canned speeches about going out into the big new world or college (every cadet attended college), etc., etc. Then, following the tradition of West Point and the Naval Academy (there was no Air Force Academy then), we all—except me—threw out caps high up in the air and cheered—I tossed mine just a few feet up and caught it because I treasured anything military and wanted to have pictures taken at home with me wearing it. I guess things like that didn't mean anything to the others. I had planned up until the end of the war the preceding year to attend the Naval Academy—what with all my naval interests fully developing at Bolles. However, with no urgent cause now, I decided to go to Yale and study art. So, off went my application to the Yale Professional School of Painting—and off I went to spend a carefree summer before knuckling down again to studies.

Chapter 16

But first:

Flying lessons

Amid the parties and activities out at the Yacht Club (we did not have a boat but many of my friends did), and the dances, and dates we double-dated on...there was never a dull moment.

Even so, I managed to work in something that my Dad and I planned to take effect before we spilled it to my Mother: Flying lessons.

Dad drove me out to a small airfield west of Jacksonville and checked me in for lessons. The sixteen million "GIs" from the war were coming home now and flooding the job market that had not yet really adjusted to peace time and many were aviators, hence many good flight instructors.

Next thing I knew I was walking around a bright yellow high-winged Piper Cub (like I had taken my first airplane ride in back in Tampa) that was constructed just like the model airplanes I made and the light canvas covering of the fuselage, wings, and tail sort of smelling like that banana glue I used—perhaps though it was the gasoline fumes.

After instruction on what everything was—which I could have told the instructor myself—he helped me get in the back seat and showed me how to strap in then did the same for himself in the seat in front of me. Then shouting to the man in front ready to crank the propeller—"Switch off"...for the man to turn the propeller to prime the engine, who shouted back, "Contact"—the pilot returned "Switch on" turning the magnetos on—the propeller stuttered, the engine coughed and the blades began to turn—then quickly spun so fast they became invisible. The instructor released the brakes, gunned the motor a bit and we started to taxi out onto the runway...he looked every-which-a-way then really gunned the motor and off we went...into the wild blue yonder.

We had no inter-phone communications, he just turned his head and raised his thumb and I got the message that I was to take over...which meant that I grabbed the "Joy" stick with my right hand and put my two feet on the left and right rudder pedals. He then made a turning motion with his hand and I tilted the stick to the right as I applied a little pressure on the right foot pedal that made the rudder on the tail move to the right taking the little plane in that direction...

I was flying!—me! Myself! Oh, what a thrill!...

We landed and did the whole thing all over again. At the next secession, he taught me how to land and I'm sure kept his own hand on the stick he used to correct any mistake I might have made. One thing we had to remember to do as we came in for a landing in such a small plane while pulling gently back on the gas throttle mounted on the left window frame was to switch the carburetor heater next to it to the 'On' position. Even though we were in a small, light airplane going at an air speed of about 70 miles per hour at an altitude of 300 feet when starting the descent, the air got cold enough to freeze up the venturi tube in the carburetor and the engine would stop—a thing that would get you to the ground too quick—and not altogether pleasantly!

After the third hour of practice, when we landed, the instructor got out and turned to me and said—"All yours" and walked away.

"All *MINE!*" Age 18 and soloing as a pilot. A dream come true...and only after three hours instruction. I lived up to the instructor's expectations and flew like a pro...going in circles over the airport at about a thousand feet, then descending with skill and remembering to flip on the carburetor heater...and made a smooth three-pointer—which means you allow the landing speed of about 40 miles per hour to stall by pulling slightly back on the stick to slightly elevate the nose just about the time the wheels touch the ground so that the tail wheel touches that same time as the two fronts ones do. *I was a natural.*

I was in seventh or tenth heaven—I lost count.

We told Mother who took it in stride, and I flew as much as I could afford that summer, at $5 per hour. I flew other types of small single-engine airplanes. They were very simple to operate, especially since there was no radio traffic then and very few other planes in the air.

One real venture I made was to fly a seaplane off the river. I had about ten hours experience then, so I trotted on down to a dock beside the big Acosta bridge where there was a flying service that had two Taylorcraft types on pontoons. Everything about them was the same as the Piper except the seats were side-by-side, with the pilot on the left. Also, there was the little matter of taking off and landing on water—quite different from terra firma. After a checkout flight, the instructor got out and I was good to go.

Remembering every detail he instructed, I taxied out away from the dock, headed down river and revved her up...picking up speed, I eased the plane 'up on the step' (so the pontoons rode like a boat hull on top of the water)...sensing that I was at the proper angle, I pulled back on the wheel (not a stick this time) and lifted off the water.

Now I gotta tell you—that was thrilling.

I flew at about two hundred feet, since the thousand foot altitude you at least had to maintain over land did not apply over water...so I skimmed along like a lark...near sailboats...and around in front of our home on the Southside...and had just a grand old time.

On the return leg, I flew a hundred feet or so off the water right toward the Acosta bridge that towered over me and did a smart left turn and settled down almost in front of the dock where I was to park— or *moor,* as in this case.

Before the summer ended, I took a Piper Cub up to about three thousand feet...flew along then abruptly pulled back on the stick and as the little Cub nosed up, kicked the right rudder pedal then wheeled over and downward in a thrilling tail-spin! I let her spin for two or three revolutions before pushing the stick straight down to straighten her out before gently pulling back to level flight. I was Errol Flynn in "Dawn Patrol" or "Eddie Rickenbacker" fighting the "Flying Circus." I did the maneuver just the way the instructor had demonstrated to me. I knew at that moment that a part of my life would be as a pilot (but it did not turn out that way).

My certificate upon soloing

Chapter 17

The College years

By the summer of 1946, the sixteen million men and women of the wartime armed forces were being released in a flood of job-seekers into a readjusting economy—it was chaos. The "GI Bill" would afford a majority of them free education in partial payment for their service—and did they jump on that! (I did so, too, for graduate school after the Korean War). Colleges and universities were inundated with applicants. Thus, my application to the professional School of Painting at Yale University came back as a 17th on the waiting list for next year, 1947. Devastating! Quickly my Dad, who had attended Sewanee Military Academy during World War I and then the University of the South (Sewanee) made a telephone call and I was off, instead, to that quaint southern institution on a mountain top in east Tennessee. Unrealized at the time, that was the best thing that could have happened to me: I took a complete academic course (since Sewanee offered no art). So, I took English Literature, Modern World History, Spanish (in which I got a grade of 100), economics (which I failed), and some sort of math.

The Sewanee experience was just like in the movies that had formed my image of college: the quasi-Gothic architecture, the isolated campus, the faculty always dressed in coats and tie and black academic gowns like at Oxford, I assumed—and, most memorably—all seniors wore academic gowns to classes, too (without the mortar board hats, though). It was all-male with probably half my Class of 1950 veterans; I recall a fraternity brother had been a Marine major and flyer. There was the customary fraternity row lining the main street of the campus, the single roadway that came from the tiny town of Monteagle through the campus and down the mountain into the valley. My friends—a number from Jacksonville—joined Phi Delta Theta—but since my Dad had been Sigma Alpha Epsilon, I joined that—a mistake due to the fact that most were all jocks and at that point I was about 5-feet six and weighed in a 118 pounds. However, I did surprise them by joining the boxing team, in what must have been a lighter-than-air-featherweight class. I did mix it up pretty well; if not power, at least I had style. I must admit, though, in a match with the local prep school, my opponent caught me with one right in the jaw—and I tell you, "I saw stars!" Stars just like those drawn in comic strips along with the hyped words: POW! WOW! SPLAT! etc.

There was a Flying Club at Sewanee, so I joined right up. The airport was down the valley in a cow pasture outside of the village of Cowan. There was the usual Piper Cub, Aeronca, a couple of others and a former Navy bi-wing Stearman trainer. In my check-out flight in a Cub with the instructor in the front seat, as I came in for the landing, I performed a 'slide-slip', meaning giving opposite rudder for a right bank which caused the plane to drop slightly sideways at a steeper angle—as we passed over a road at the end of the field—and, of course, I remembered to turn the carburetor heater on—and pulled up to gently stall for a perfect three-point landing—getting a passing grade from the somewhat startled instructor who had instinctively grabbed onto a window strut when I side-slipped.

Back in my dorm room I decided to do a barrel-roll and so sat in a chair and practiced and practiced coordinating the controls for a roll.

I guess I took a bus down the valley and rented an Aeronca and took it up to four thousand feet—out of sight of the airport. Flying along steady, observing the air in all directions around me...I girded myself and started my practiced moves: I nosed downward a bit to pick up speed...tilted back up and then abruptly flipped the stick over to the right to roll...I rolled alright—but crazy-like—the nose went up too steeply, then down—gas spewed out of the gauge in front of the windscreen—wind whined loudly in the tensing wing struts—there were a series of audible stresses and strains throughout as I tried to bring her back to level flight. When I finally did after the few seconds that seemed to me to have been an hour struggling with the stick and rudder pedals...I had to fly around calmly for a half hour before my heart returned to its regular beat and my hand stopped shaking. Fortunately the Aeronca was a bit sturdier than the Piper.

In all, I accumulated 35 hours on my log book before I gave up flying. And, the reason I did so was not my aerobatic attempts but the cost of flying: that $5 an hour. I had to make a decision; was I going to have dates come up from Jacksonville on special weekends and spend money on that—or fly?

The feminine gender triumphed over the call of adventure.

Shortly after my momentous decision to resign from the Flying Club due to lack of money, that allowed for a weekend date. So, good friend Hugh Powell from Bolles and I invited two girls up from Jacksonville: I invited gorgeous Mary Jo Stroud and Hugh, gorgeous Edith Guernsey. There was a dance of course and some fraternity activities and a good time was had by all—a fond memory.

Mary Jo, Hugh, and Edith

"Over the sea, let's go men..."

An event occurred that affected my life from that day forward: A Marine Corps recruiter came on campus. Naturally I knew all about the Marines and how they had won the Pacific war and I wanted to be just like John Wayne when he took Iwo Jima, as I have always told the story—until I found out to my chagrin that that movie was made two years later than when I joined the officers' program at Sewanee, the Marine Corps Reserve Platoon Leaders' Class (PLC).

> NOTE: I had no idea of the fierce struggle going on in Washington at the time about restructuring all the armed forces and eliminating the Marine Corps. (I wrote extensively about that in my monumental "Semper Fi: the Definitive Illustrated History of the U.S. Marines" published by Barnes&Noble in 2005, 2010) Much less that I would go to war in the Marines three times and rise to the rank of colonel—a thing I devoutly would have wished but could not conceive then of ever happening, not in those wind-down days of that recent big war.

Marine Platoon Leaders' Class trainee
Chenoweth in Summer Training

The upshot was that I reapplied to the Yale School of Painting and, in the meantime, my parents had looked into my attending the Yale Summer Art School. I was all for that!

Art School—*par excéllence*: Summer of '47 in Connecticut

The six-week Yale Summer Art School alternated with the six-month Yale Summer Music School in the charming New England village of Norfolk, Connecticut, situated in the picturesque northwest corner of the state amid the rolling piedmont of the Berkshires and beautiful Haystack mountain.

It seems my life just couldn't get any better. I traveled up by train, way up to Canaan, I guess, where a bus from the school awaited me and a few others who were headed there. The school was a very large (no more "Bigs") one-story house with a sweeping front porch. Inside was a lounge area, a meeting area, and a dining area; this would be our headquarters. In some other nearby buildings were the art/music studios and possibly some dorm rooms. I, however, was paired off with three other guys and we had rented rooms in a house down the road. The owner was a nice elderly lady who took us in as "Her Boys," which suited us fine. Someone must have had a car; I really don't recall how we got back and forth.

Once registration and the get-acquainted period was over, we purchased our art supplies from the in-house store. One of the items I bought, of course, was a large wooden paint box, the lid of which opened and had an inside rack to hold one or two canvas boards and separated sections for tubes of paint and little bottles of turpentine and linseed oil. Would you believe?—after sixty-eight years, I still have that box and use it—dried caked paint still on the palette.

To my sheer delight, the classes began outdoors on the campus where we would paint "Alla Prima," that is, directly onto the canvas boards as the modernists chose to do, rather than the Old Masters' time-consuming technique of executing a monochromatic underpainting and then layering thin transparent color glazes over and over until the right color effect was achieved (This was still taught in the Yale School of Painting at its main campus in New haven—as I was to find out that Fall). I much preferred this fresh, direct approach.

One of the classes advanced my burgeoning maturity: a "Life" class. As I was setting up my easel and squeezing the basic paints out of their tubes onto my palette, out walked a naked woman! No one blinked but me! I had never seen a naked—*nude*—woman up that close before (the only other one I had ever seen was when Bolles classmate Charlie Krueger and I were at the beach house and had just turned out our bedroom light when a light flicked on in a window of the very close house next door and at our same second floor level. We both naturally turned in that direction—and lo and behold—what any boy of that—or any age would give anything to watch happened: a beautiful young lady walked into the just lighted room, went to the mirror to preen a bit...and then began disrobing! Our eyes just about came out of their sockets!

Unaware of her two admirers just a few yards away—in the adjoining yard—she did a languorous—to us wide-eyed sightseers—and —to us if we could have articulated the word: provocative strip-tease that I can still recall from minute to minute. Neither of us quite realized what new stirrings were taking place in our loins during this— but nothing averted our intense attention until she flicked her light out. *Oh...such days of innocence.*

But, this was not a strip-tease, this wondrously nude lady just came out like it was nothing at all and posed herself unashamedly on a stool in front of us—*me*! I was totally flustered but tried not to show it...so I perfunctorily went about mixing my paints and wondering how to start —sneaking a quick peek now and then a those unfamiliar and heretofore hidden parts of the female anatomy—*these*—not pictures but the real thing!

The effect was not quite like my first kiss but the image stayed with me for many days afterward...and we drew or painted her several times thereafter...and I got used to seeing a nude woman and the pleasant shock began to wear off. (I can tell you—such a pleasant sight is a lasting one—and it never diminishes)

The whole experience of the Summer Art School was glorious. All the young guys and gals were wonderful—and terribly talented. I had never been in such brilliant company and relished it. We partied and picnicked, had dances, drank some beer and did some innocent (I suppose) 'necking' (Oh, that Loris Lapidus!). One stupid thing we did, though, was one night a group of us drove in somebody's car down to a small lake to go swimming, so we had on bathing attire. Someone challenged us all to swim across the lake and back. I was a pretty good swimmer, so went along...with some trepidation, since there was no moon and anything could happen—especially if someone got a cramp. I had "Life Guard" certification for the Church day camp back a few years ago—so, we all plunged in an stroked off for the other shore. As always, the other shore is farther than it seems, and this proved true. And, in the dark we could only make contact by voice.

In short, everyone made it over and back, but that taught me a lesson in foolishness: avoid it in the future.

One of the best experiences was an outdoor jaunt in the nearby woods beside another lake to paint right from nature. We went down a dirt road and came to the site (which, no doubt, was painted by many each year—but so what!) This was a first for me. I set up my easel and this time a larger stretched canvas to paint on. And, so paint I did—*en plein air*. In an hour or so I had my 'masterpiece' that stood up to the work of the other students—we were all pretty good—no beginners.

When it ended, we all departed sadly, having made very good acquaintances during our session, although I did not keep up with any of the others afterward. (*Goodby, again, Loris Lapidus!*)

On to Ol' Elihu YALE, the Whiffenpoofs, *et al.—so I thought*!

Back home—to find that I had been accepted to Yale for the coming year. My reapplication to Sewanee was rescinded and off I went to New Haven.

After Sewanee, the Yale campus was overpowering. Due to the continuing influx of veterans and the fact that I was in a Professional School, not Yale College, I had to board in temporary housing in the athletic field house, in a cubicle with a bed, chair, and mirror, and a cloth curtain for privacy. This was not quite the Ivy League experience I had envisioned. Although not necessarily needed, as my grandfather was paying my tuition (back then, as now, the price of tuition was about the same as a medium sized-automobile), I decided to work in the cafeteria slopping hash from the hot plates. I did this for only a very short time.

I befriended a guy from California, who was not the usual Ivy League type—a little too Hollywood sporty but he had a car, a convertible, and he took a couple of us guys around. One day, though, when I was the only one with him, we came to a corner stop—but he didn't and turned into a coming car from our left—that resulted in a fender-bender. A ticket was issued and a court date was made for his appearance. The accident was totally his fault, but he tried to prevail on me to testify that he had, indeed, stopped and that it was the other driver's fault. Unhesitatingly, I refused; he got fined and never spoke to me again—but I figured no loss. Several times in later life I have been faced with such a situation and have preserved my integrity by refusing and distancing myself. In so doing I may have lost friends or opportunities but I certainly felt better.

As to the art classes, they were a big disappointment. All morning we had to make little puddles of paint in various hues, values, and intensities; in the afternoon, we drew in charcoal from plaster casts of heads—a bust of Voltaire being the most used—and molds of hands and those sorts of things. I began to think that if this is what I would be doing for the next five years (since I had to start over as a freshman in this program), that this was for the birds!

The proverbial straw that broke the camel's back was a class in design. The "Professor" had us draw some curved lines in a rectangle.

I drew mine and instinctively added a little counter-curved accent that seemed to be needed. When the professor graded them, he held mine up and examined it, then thought a bit, picked out my little added fillip and then pronounced that this deserved a...and he paused...an "80."

Thank god I'd had an academic year at Sewanee! That was pure nonsense—giving me a numerical grade on a bunch of lines! An "80" based on what criteria? I said to myself, "That's it!" and went right to the telephone to call my folks and tell them to get me out of there. If I could not transfer to Yale College—and I found out I could not—then I wanted to go back to Sewanee.

To see how Fate works its mysterious ways, the person at Sewanee who answered my Dad's call said they were all filled up and could not take another student; so my grandfather called his brother, Herbert's lawyer son, William Avery, in Chicago, who had graduated from Princeton and was still on its board, to see if he could get me into Princeton—two weeks late in my sophomore year. (After I got into Princeton, a Sewanee professor who knew my father called and said he had just heard that I had been turned down for reentry—and he was appalled. Had my Dad talked to him I would have gone back there. The Fate part is that had I done so, my entire life would have been different; I might never have gone to New York, the Marines, done my art, written books, married that tall girl—or ended up where I am now, satisfied in my retirement. So, I have learned not to tempt Fate—leave things to it (him or whomever).

Uncle Bill (a noted lawyer) arranged an interview for me right away down at Princeton in New Jersey and I took a train there immediately.

194

I had the interview and because Princeton had not filled its regional quota for the Southeast, and my being from Jacksonville and with a good freshman year from Sewanee—or maybe the fact that they relished a transfer from Yale (but I kid myself not: it was mostly from my uncle's word), I was accepted. Joyfully, I returned to Yale, resigned or terminated or whatever, packed my things and even stopped to tell that professor that I had transferred to Princeton. He knew that Princeton had an excellent Art History department. I resisted telling him what I thought of his teaching and the Yale School of Painting.

Princeton: "Old Nassau"

An acrylic painting I did of Blair Archway in the 1970s for a series about campus activities.

I had no trouble settling into my third college in two years, this time in a private room in the top floor of Foulke Hall, overlooking the famous Blair Hall archway. I could hardly believe it. Now, really in the "Ivy League!" The professional school of painting at Yale was not really considered "Ivy League"—and I was quite aware of that, not that it mattered at the time. But when I became a part of Princeton, my head swelled pridefully. I walked around the startlingly beautiful campus and identified those spots where the photographs had recently accompanied a laudatory article in *Colliers*, I think it was. Good grief! Here I was!

I was very fortunate to be assigned to a private room, right on the top floor of Foulke Hall, overlooking Holder Archway.

Now, to classes:

I had arrived two weeks late in my sophomore year, having had no academic work on that level at all at Yale. I was to find right off the bat that that made no difference to any of my Princeton professors; I was expected to plunge right in a make up the preceding two weeks work and be prepared for the upcoming tests—I was cut no slack. How I managed was by not thinking about it and hitting the books—*hard*; thank goodness for the Sewanee experience. I took the Art & Archaeology major, which meant a bunch of art courses, in addition to which, I also took French, and later Spanish and German, plus literature, music appreciation, philosophy, and accounting courses.

In the art courses I was especially in my element; I did well in the others with the exception of accounting. By today's standards, the art course materials were terribly primitive. This was 1947, mind you, and the whole art world was in transition; transition from the pre-war years with the semi-absorption of so-called modern trends: Impressionism, Expressionism, Cubism, and the rest, which the war had more or less suspended. Following the war, the art cognoscenti—and by this, I mean the professors, the museum curators, the art critics, as well as students —were all in limbo. There was no particular "Art Movement" of the 1940s. Even the Yale and Princeton professors were not quite sure of Picasso's place in art history as yet, as he was still very much alive. Both institutions were dragging their feet in leaving comfortable traditional realism to step boldly forward—and they foresaw nothing to step forward into, despite the 1920s European Bauhaus modernizing movement, the following Art Deco, and other peripheral movements. Part of the reason was limited communication; news of innovative art trends came out first in European or U.S. magazines—and who really was to judge? The editors, the critics, the academicians, or the artists?

Fortunately from the art history point of view, I was fortunate to some degree; but from the creative (there was an extra-curricular painting and sculpture class or two) standpoint, the merely academic studio still-lifes and figure studies were stale, stultifying stuff.

Six years after I graduated and earned my Master of Fine Arts in Painting at the University of Florida, the "Abstract-Expressionist" art movement had exploded on the art world in New York and that had been subsumed by the art department at the U. of Fla. into which I had plunged myself in 1954 (with wife and baby on the way). "Academic met Abstract"—and 'ere the two did meet was much consternation— until the latter finally got through to me as valid. I had been a bit stand-offish with this new movement, but when I came to understand pre-World War I artist Paul Klee's observation that art now did not have to be reflective of nature but could be a creation on a surface that stood alone as art, it penetrated my thick head...and I was off and running. And, earned my MFA in 1956.

Still, there were no great art images in the Princeton art department from which to study; they were all either black & white of faded color prints mounted on grey cardboard and arranged on wall racks to study. There were few art books then with color reproductions and the art instruction was generally dull and stogy. Had I not been an artist myself, I probably wound not have stuck with it. There was only one other art major who was artistic; the rest were simply there to take a "gut" course (to them) or were destined for museum curatorship. This is one reason I have so little regard for art dealers, gallery owners, and curators: they only know what they have learned from others—not what an artist gleans instinctively from art by creating art himself.

But, I digress. I was what one would have called an "incurable Romantic," in the classical sense back then. It was not in my mind to prepare for the real world but to live vicariously in the cultural one of art, music, and languages—more of a dilettante, if I had stopped to think about it. Of course, influenced greatly by the movies of those times, they formed my concept of the world to a large degree. I envisioned myself sitting in a Paris café pontificating in three languages about the arts while sipping apéritif after apéritif. (I did manage part of this delusion after the Korean War when I did live on the Left Bank in Paris for a short time; however, my artistic endeavors then were sidetracked by a good bit of socializing with a conglomerate of foreign students with the same ideas.

A missed moment

Don't we all at one time or another have a "missed moment"? When, after a meeting, an encounter, an event, we slap our heads and say, "Why the devil didn't I say that?"

Well, one day as I entered the Art classroom building, McCormick Hall, coming down the stairs but hidden from me by a wall, I could clearly heard a male voice singing *"Depuis le jour..."*—and he stopped as I came around the corner. I could have finished the line since I knew that aria from the opera Louise from my grandmother's recording "... *ou je me suis donnée...."* Shy me—I just looked up at him and exchanged smiles and went on. That silly missed encounter has bugged me all my life. There I was, a young neophyte student and could have astounded an erudite professor by not missing a beat and finishing the line for him. Wouldn't THAT have been a coup? But—I missed it. I have been kicking myself (mentally) ever since.

One little kudo I won right off was first prize in a student art exhibit. It was a corny little stylized gouache painting of a negro cabin in the South with the family and kids and a dog romping. A black & white scratchboard drawing I had done for the Sewanee Review in my Freshman year, entitled "Damn, you, Papiols!" depicted Bertrand de Borne lashing out as Dante had confined him to the eighth rung of Hades in his *Inferno* and poet Ezra Pound had picked up on it in his "Sestina Altaforte." I got paid by the Princeton art museum the *princely* sum of twenty-five dollars and it supposedly went into its permanent student art collection.

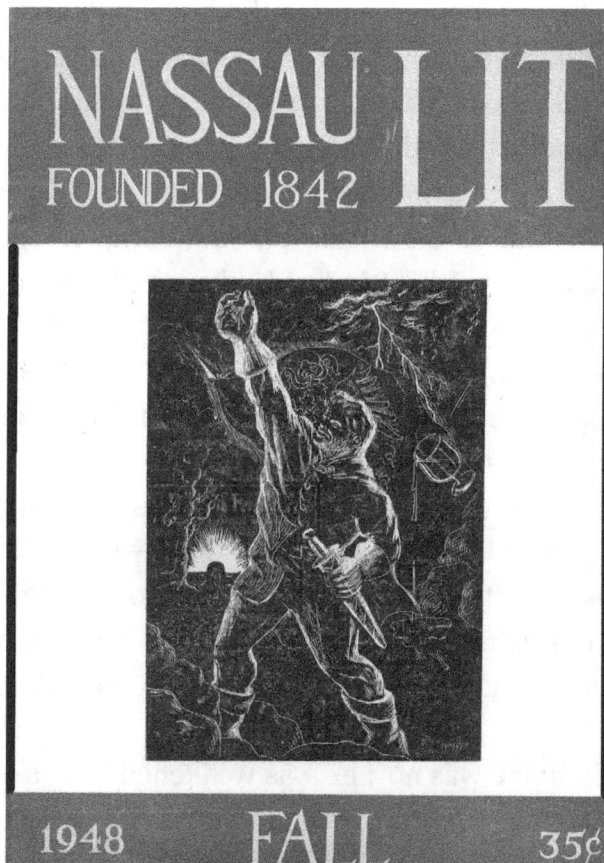

*This scratchboard was also used on
the* Sewanee Review *the previous year.*

Distressing news

During the fall of my junior year distressing news came from home: my Dad had suffered a cerebral hemorrhage. He was 48 years old and it was 1948. I was devastated not knowing what that meant nor what would happen to the family and then to me? Would my Dad pull through? Would I be able to stay at Princeton? Should I return home? How long would he be in the hospital? I was understandably unnerved.

Fortunately, my grandfather would continue the tuition payments, which amounted to $2,500 per year, roughly the same price as a good automobile then. (That is about the same today: a $50,000 tuition and a $50,000 automobile)

Sometime later, after he got out of the hospital but with the loss of control of his right side, arm, and leg, and his speech so blurred he could not be understood (indicating damage to the left side of the brain). His doctor advised that he undergo an unique operation done at the Yale medical center in New Haven. Now—mind you—he was to go alone in his condition on a train to New York, change trains from Pennsylvania Station on the West side, hail and take a taxi—with a suitcase—over to Grand Central Station, buy a ticket, and await a train to New Haven—a tricky and exhausting feat even for a well person.

Poor guy...he made it but in worsened condition. The operation, I think it was called a cervical sympathectomy, was done and my Mother called to ask me to go up to New Haven and see him—and put him on the train back home. I don't now how I did it—but I did get to New Haven. He looked quite normal following the operation (of course, I had not seen him exhibiting the effects of the stroke). So I got him homeward bound and reported that the operation seemed very successful.

Well, the trip home was not; he was weakened by the operation and really had been in no condition to travel at all. It would have been far better had someone driven a car up there to not only take him but to bring him back home. My grandfather had too many duties to attend to but my Mother could easily have done so. I wondered why. By the time he got home he was as bad off as before.

An oil portrait I painted of my Father from life in 1955, seven years after his stroke.

My Dad's physical impairments prevented him from taking over the warehouse business but he did eventually go to work each day, dragging his right leg and cradling his right arm and able to utter enough words to be understood. It was frustrating, though, for him to have his thoughts but not be able to express them. Sadly, we were both robbed of any Father-Son closeness from thence on. I could tell, though, that he comprehended and relished in his own silent world the accomplishments I made, my marriage, and the arrival of his grandchildren, before he died twenty years later.

An acrylic I did of Reunions also in the 1970s for the cover of the Princeton Alumni Weekly *magazine*

The Princeton "Experience"

That's the only way to put it: *Experience*. It was a world unto itself. A cocoon of cultural, intellectual, artistic, and creative factions that became the glorious essence of what college was all about. The ambience was a far cry from what it is today: it was all-male then, the faculty for the most part had served in the war, and many were famous for their works before the war, hence more into the past (I guess as historians should rightly be), but the climate—the intellectual climate was less toward the future than one might have expected—at least from my perspective—and on the Liberal Arts side, far from any preparation for the real world ahead. The greatest thing about the experience was the quiet time one had to one's self...time to sit under a tree and read or meditate with no distractions. Or, join in a polite conversation and learn something serendipitously to feed that burgeoning polymathic dimension to one's course curricula. Compared to today's campus life at Princeton or anywhere else, the 1940s were, again, simple, slow-paced, and allowed for digestive contemplation. Granted, there were more mature students than today with veterans returning from the war on the "GI" bill that paid their tuition, housing, and books.

The ambience on campus was genteel. No one dressed sloppily—all dressed what pejoratively today would be called "Preppy," tan chinos, loafers without socks, regular long sleeved shirts with buttoned-down collars—even in hot weather, these with sleeves rolled up rather than more comfortable Tee shirts. Sport coats were favored over outdoor jackets—with a large wool scarf for colder weather. And, pullover sweaters.

Almost all of the upperclassmen (juniors and seniors) joined "eating clubs" just off campus on "Club Row." Unlike Greek-letter fraternities at public and other colleges, these were well-kept and orderly mansions lining Prospect Street. Having come as a sophomore, I missed Freshman orientation and my Class of 1950 friend-making. Consequently, I was a bit on the periphery. Fortunately, several of my classmates from Bolles were already there: Quinn Barton, Nick Canaday, Karl Madson, and Fred Schultz, who was to delay and join the next year's class. But, as to the Clubs, those supposedly the most prestigious were filled with the wealthier northern prep school types from Exeter, Andover, Groton, and Choate prep schools; many were from famous multi-millionaire families. Before the war that was a more important factor in admissions but with the influx of war veterans, that notched down a peg or two. I was fortunately befriended by another outsider who was a bit older but was able to get me shooed into one of the clubs, "Key & Seal" down at the end of club row.

Once in a club, you were obligated to take evening dinner there and be dressed accordingly, in coat and tie. The atmosphere was most gentlemanly. We all sat at separate table-clothed tables and were waited on by uniformed waiters (mostly negro). Following that rather formal dining, we then retired to the living room where we were brought cups of after-dinner coffee and enjoyed polite conversation (Could you envision THAT today?). Upstairs in the pool room was a large black & white television set. In about 1948 or '49, television programs began televising out of New York for a limited number of hours during early evening, at the end of which there would be a visual and musical rendition of the Star-Spangled Banner signal 'sign-off'.

One highlight of those early experimental days of TV was "Your Show of Shows" hosted by a hilarious comedian, Sid Caesar, and NBC's "Texaco Star Theater," starring another comedian, Milton Berle.. There were others, too, with Metropolitan Opera stars and such. (Little did I know then that within three years from graduation, I, too, would be IN television—in a pioneering local TV station in Jacksonville as a director —even before the transcontinental cable connected the East and West coasts with a single national system).

At the clubs on Party Weekends, there was a lot of beer drinking— both Princetonians and their attractive dates. A few got in their cups but nothing like what goes on in today's colleges—and even now at Princeton. Occasionally on campus there would be a late night cry to storm Renwicks, a restaurant on Nassau Street, and restless students would pile out from their studying and congregate on Nassau Street and act like they were rioting. A pane of glass would get broken and the crowd would disperse—and a bill would be sent to the class responsible to pay for damages. This, a far cry from the nude streaking across campus by both male and female students there in recent times.

A Night at the Opera

When studies were over and it was not a party weekend, I'd take the train to the big city to visit museums, art galleries, and concerts. By very good fortune, a distant older cousin had an apartment on the upper East Side and he gave me the key to use on the weekends when he and his 'partner' went to their cottage in upstate New York. Can't beat a deal like that!

So, this young Romantic would up an go to spend a spartan weekend with probably one highlight being a Broadway play, an opera, or a museum trek.

I was so enthralled at one opera performance at the old 39th Street Metropolitan Opera House, that I asked how I could BE in one myself. I was told to come around the following Friday in late afternoon and go around the corner to the stage door entrance and tell the man at the door you wanted to be a supernumerary in that night's opera. I did so and was told to go three floors down (underground) and see the wardrobe department. There, I was handed a clump of costume—that of an ancient Egyptian soldier. It reeked to high heaven—sweat, mildew, rancid whatever...and I dutifully put it on—looking absolutely ridiculous (not like a Bolles 'soldier' or a Marine). Other people of various sorts were doing the same thing, Then I overheard a conversation with the crowd master that there were not enough supernumeraries for the crowd scenes—and an order to go across the street to the bars over there and grab some who were not too drunk and bring them back. All they would have to do is don a robe and wander around with the others up stage in the crowd scene.

We got up backstage somehow and the next step was to get in step as we were assembled into a line of double ranks. You could hear the singers out on the stage very clearly—and I recognized the music (and already knew the name of the opera). The stage manager then got the long line of us to step in rhythm with the music and to the count of a march...when that famous march began, we began our left-right steps to it right out onto the stage of the great Metropolitan Opera House in a cadence   all school graduates are familiar with: the "Triumphal March" of the second act of Verdi's famed opera "Aïda." We were Radames' triumphant returning soldiers aligning ourselves in front of a grand Egyptian temple. Radames, himself, was mounted on a white steed—yes, right there on stage. I guess he dismounted as we marched behind the singers—with one Egyptian soldier out of step—*Me!* I'd been gawking at the resplendent jeweled boxes lining the several-tiered balconies of the famed "Diamond Horseshoe" that, indeed, did glitter from all the *Glitterrati.*

Once in place, the performance was a *gas*! The prompter in the tiny shell at the front of the stage floor just behind the foot-lights had a large book spread on the stage in front of him to which he had his eyes glued (figuratively), reading the entire libretto just ahead of the singers. He would come to a spot, put his finger on it, and raise his other and look straight into the eyes of the next singer. When he was sure of that singer's attention, he hesitated—and just before cueing the words with a hand gesture—he shouts them out so all the singers on the stage could hear him—but the audience could not: "CE-le-es-te a-Ï-DA...FOR-ma-a di-VI-na...MIS-ti-i-co REG-gio..."—then point at the singer at the precise moment of entry. In the meantime, on stage behind Radames and Aïda, whenever a male singer—including Radames himself—turned his back to the audience, he would wink at one of the female supers—or if, knowing he could not be seen, sneak a quick pinch at a fanny. It was fascinating to uncover this bit of foolishness that went unsuspected by the high-falutin' "Diamond Horseshoe" élite, white-tie-and-tails crowd out front—many of whom perhaps did not enjoy opera nearly as much as I did.

While on this musical theme, I managed to see Italian-American composer Cian Carlo Menotti's two Broadway operettas: the "Medium" and "The Telephone." Both were sensational hits and after their New York run, Menotti was to take them to London (this must have been in the Spring of 1950). My strange friend-mentor (of sorts) who, was an opera as well as an art buff, and who had gotten me into the eating club at Princeton, happened to be a friend of Menotti's. And, Menotti was throwing a going-away party at the Plaza hotel in NY and had invited my friend—who then invited me.

So, up I went to the City and to the apartment. Nearing the appointed time for dinner, I began to make my way across Manhattan from East 51st Street (and under the East side elevated railway tracks still there back then) cutting diagonally over to Fifth Avenue. Approaching Fifth on 58th Street, I came to the Savoy Plaza hotel; surely, I thought, this must be what was colloquially called "The *Plaza.*" Without giving it another thought, I entered its lobby...and was a bit confused because it was not very impressive. Anyway, I paced around awaiting the appointed hour and my friend and Menotti to show up.

Time passed...more time—a whole hour...and I began to worry. Finally, spotting the big structure beyond the small park in front of the Plaza I was in, I asked the man behind the desk what it was. He said, "That's the *PLAZA.*"

I gulped and high-tailed it, darting across traffic and into the magnificent lobby of the real and famous Plaza Hotel. After a while my friend showed up and asked where the hell I'd been. Sheepishly I admitted across the street (oh, me, such a neophyte and country-boy still!).

He dragged me over to the elevator and up we went to Menotti's room, which was bulging with people—all sorts of people, obviously from the theater, fashion, the arts (not a one like a Princetonian).

I was briefly introduced to Menotti and praised his two works which I had seen (and could quote the opening lines of The Telephone). Whereupon, on taking our leave, my friend astonished me by kissing Menotti fully on the lips as a farewell. (This confirmed a suspicion of mine, which is why I dane to mention my friend's name here).

At least that is a true story out of which I have gotten a lot of mileage. Menotti later created the Spoleto Music Festival in Charleston, South Carolina.

Musical anecdote:

Always one to choose talent over beauty—but more than ever delighted to find both—I had somehow met a very talented and beautiful young lady down the road in Trenton. Her talent was the most wonderful lyric soprano voice I had ever heard up close—for she sang a few clips of arias to enthrall me. And she was (as one says nowadays) 'drop-dead gorgeous'!

Since I had no car or means to go to Trenton and date her, except the bus, an opportunity presented itself on a special weekend. I must have prevailed on her to have her father drive her over—no matter, she arrived at my Key & Seal club. There we joined the fun and frolic and maybe some beer drinking. But, it was at lunch that the event occurred.

She (and I forget her name—I can't remember them ALL!)—and I were sitting at one of the dining tables by the mullioned gothic window looking out on Prospect Street, enjoying a 'swell-elegant' lunch...when a dowager all dolled up like Park Avenue's best on Easter Sunday asked if she could join us; there were no other seats available.

Being the gracious gentleman that I always am, I got up and drew a chair back and held it for her to sit. Best of manners; befitting a proper Princtonian, eh what?

Well, the pleasantries began and the conversation was refined and she told about her son there, whom I knew casually...and I, of course, brought up the fact of my date's marvelous singing voice and operatic ability, which caused Mrs. Social Register's eyes to gleam a bit being in the presence of two such charming and engaging young people.

Then my date broke in excitedly to tell about a dream that she had recently had—that her father would soon be given a very high position. I smiled and so did the dowager, who must have anticipated something along the lines of a Wall Street promotion, or a Captain of Industry, a Cabinet Post...something well in her league.

My lovely, ingenuous date went on to explain that, yes, it really happened: her father just received a high promotion—he was elevated to chief crane operator!

Mrs. South Hampton's jaw dropped, her mouth agape a bit un-ladylike, her eyes widened and she blinked—as she suddenly moved back in her chair, got up, nodded to us condescendingly, and walked away.

My date merely looked puzzled, but I knew perfectly well class conceit for what it was—and I would have bet my pedigree topped hers.

As to my date, I would have been proud to take her anywhere. She was poised, articulate, and that voice of hers was a gift of the gods. I never saw her again, and unfortunately, I can't recall her name; she could have made it big in opera, the stage, or motion pictures. Park Avenue be damned!

But, then again, Park Avenue raised its beautiful head again when I met another wonderful girl who actually did live on Park Avenue, and she was attending Mount Holyoke College at the time. How we met escapes me but a group of us went up to visit her and some of her girl friends in her apartment there and I invited her down for party weekends. This turned out to be the real thing: I fell in love. Her name was Heather Roulston. She was my date for graduation when she met my family and things were sort of assumed from there on out. But, that's another story—interrupted by a war in Korea.

Miscellany

Compared to today's teaching, in the late 1940s there was a lot left to be desired. Oh, there were famous profs and noted teachers, but one example did not turn out so well for me. I took a painting course from a well-known art historian, self-proclaimed artist, Lester Cook. Under his tutelage I learned nothing and I was a far better painter. Unfortunately, I chose him as my thesis advisor; my subject was "The Technique of Portrait Painting," of which I thought he knew something about—which, it turned out, he didn't. I researched and wrote my 100-page thesis, introducing a seminal observation about the size of the subject's head relative to the distance the subject was portrayed behind the frontal plane. As I discussed it with him a few times, he really had nothing to comment on; I naïvely attributed that to wisdom, that is, he allowing me to figure things out for myself—which I did, despite him. Furthermore, he didn't even comment on my final draft so I went to typing, printing, and binding.

Another reviewer's comments were complimentary but noted that I should have had more input from my advisor. Nevertheless, I got a passing mark (and, have probably made more money from my later portraiture than Cook ever did from his art).

This sterling professor went from Princeton to a major national museum, resting on his "laurels," certainly not his competence in my mind.

My conclusion: art historians are not artists, and artists are not pedant historians. Artists are therefore at the mercy of those who do not truly comprehend the processes of creativity and subsequently rely on perpetuating the words and ideas of those who have preceded them. Oddly, I have succeeded as both and artist and an historian.

About midway in my last senior semester, the predictable 'senior blahs' set in. I sat back and asked myself if this was all worth it? What would an art degree mean anyway? Why not just up and leave and go out in the world and begin painting? Making a name for myself?

Again, that sensible inner voice-in-my-ear won out—*fortunately!*—and I stayed and received the degree and Marine commission. As might have been imagined, back in those days and Ivy League degree was, indeed, a door-opener...and, it opened many for me. I doubt if that is as true nowadays.

I recall one of the first members of our class to actually land a real job, to commence immediately following Commencement, proudly announcing that he would be making the astounding amount of $250 per month! *WOW!*—probably shuffling papers in a big Wall Street firm. But that was pretty good back then. My net monthly paycheck in the Marine Corps the following year was $265; pretty good for a Marine lieutenant leading 85 hardened Marines against North Korean and Chinese enemy troops. That was, so to speak, my first executive job! When I entered local television in Jacksonville in 1953, my wages were $30 per week.

Breaks from Academia

A typical boat party on the St. Johns River in Jacksonville. (L to R) Mary Paula "Paubo" Armstrong, Larry Lovett, Beverly "Wookie" Register, Flo Hope Lipscomb, yours truly, and two unidentifieds but known then.

The Silver Meteor, *Whoo, Whoo!*

You leave the little "Dinky" station 'bout a quarter to four,
Get off at the Junction and wait a bit more;
Then here comes the Silver Meteor all shiny and bright,
To take you on your journey throughout the long night.
You join your classmates in the Club Car to swig a few beers,
Down way too many and start to shout vulgar cheers,
The conductor shoos you out and back to your seat.
You try to sleep it off in a twisted pretzel heap.
The dreaded morning comes and you start to awaken,
Ugly memories of the previous night leave you a bit shaken.
Then in strides the porter saying Savannah's just a short stay;
Thank god Jacksonville's only an hour or two away.
But with your heavy hangover it'll be a long day.
There's gonna be all your family waitin' at the station,
Then you think what a way to start Spring vacation!
Oh, Silver Meteor you done meteored me home...
...Slur you, with a low agonizing groan.

> Hoping the late Harry Warren and Johnny Mercer
> would pardon my doggerel.

NOTE: Travel by train was the custom; air lines were too costly and hard to get to. The station for the "Dinky's" double-car short back-and-forth to the main tracks at Princeton Junction was conveniently on campus.

When we were home from college, dating was the norm. Every guy it seems could borrow the family car and single or double-date. If it were not a "Drive-in Movie," where you could park in the darkened lot to watch the flick while necking, one would drive over to the local "Drive-in" fast food joint. (McDonalds had not been invented as yet) There you would park among other members of your 'crowd' with their dates, and, when the order gal glided up to your car window on her roller skates to take your order...she almost knew right off that it would be a grilled cheese for your date and a cheeseburger for you and two cokes with straws. (Somewhat like "American Graffiti," but without the hi-jinks)

Two of my friends at home had boats, little cabin cruiser types, and they would throw all-day boating parties on the St. Johns River or sometimes all the way down to the inland waterway canal paralleling the Atlantic coastline. Bolles and Princeton classmate, Quinn Barton (a teetotaler), owned one. Yes, there was beer and we could all handle it pretty well, often exaggerating its effect for no purpose other than to hide the fact that we had had enough. These were always fun and no harm was ever done.

There were continuous social affairs, Debutante Balls, and dances at the Yacht Club out in Ortega and at the Timmuquana Country Club, and the dancing, swimming, and partying down at the Ponte Vedra Beach Club near our cottage. A "Gay Ol' Time" was had by all—in the former *proper* meaning of that word. Yes, we were frivolous. We didn't read the newspapers, hardly ever caught the news on the radio between the plethora of songs, were oblivious of the real world to come, knowing that it was right there just waiting for us. "N'ary a care in the world." We instinctively enjoyed life as we could.

One thing that haunted me, though, was a snippet I read about Princeton statistics that cited a certain former class in which everyone was highly successful in business, medicine, finances, teaching, etc., yet four were merely hourly-wage workers.

I swore that would never happen to me.

Campus life

For my Sophomore and junior years I was fortunate to have a dormitory room all to myself. Neat freak that I was, it was always spotless and orderly, impressing friends when they stopped in. I frankly saw no reason to be sloppy. I had decent furniture that I must have picked up from somewhere: a bed, chair and a drafting table that maybe my Dad drove up to me. I also had a 78-rpm record turntable and the newly finished Firestone Library had a great musical record borrowing section; so I liked to play classical pieces when I studied. Across the hall was a Marine veteran on the GI Bill. He could not stand hearing anything when he studied—much less classical music—and he didn't buy my trying to convince him that I had to hear it for a music appreciation course. So, he'd get ticked off and go to the library to study—where he should have gone in the first place.

For my senior year, two friends of mine invited me to join them in a suite of rooms in the prestigious "'79 Hall" with its famous archway in the middle of the dormitory opening to the street of eating clubs.

Their suite had a little entrance hallway, a good-sized living room on the right with a fireplace, the off the left of the hallway were two small bedrooms with bunk beds in each.

It was too perfect to believe—just like the movies of Oxford and Cambridge—ours all in the "Collegiate Gothic" style of most of the campus. In the living room over the fireplace was draped a large Princeton banner; on the walls I could hang a few of my paintings.

Al Shands, Tom Brown, Bill Corrigan, and Ave Chenoweth

On the end wall of the little entrance hallway was a large Confederate flag (two of my roommates, Alfred Shands and Bill Corrigan were from the South, too), under which were two empty bourbon bottles with half-burned candles stuck in them (Oh, so daring!), all giving the effect of a shrine. The instigator of that was probably the fourth roommate, Tom Brown, who was quite a boozer—so much so that he died a few years after graduation from alcoholism.

Extracurricular

Having not the slightest inclination of going out for sports, I looked instead to the humor magazine as a cartoonist for the "Tiger," and the literary one, the " Nassau Lit." The campus radio station, WPRU, was also a creative outlet. I landed a hosting spot on a classical music program mainly due to the fact that I knew and could pronounce the French, German, and Italian titles; I did a fairly decent imitation of Milton Downs who still hosted the Metropolitan Opera broadcasts.

One day, when the host of the following disk-jockey program was late, I tried to imitate his jazzy, loud intro—failing embarrassingly.

(I did later go into broadcasting, both radio and television, the latter both behind and before the camera)

My panoramic acrylic of Nassau Street in the 1970 series
of paintings of the campus

The charming little town of Princeton

If the reader has never been to Princeton, New Jersey, you have missed a treat. Besides the university's idyllic campus, the town is out of a story book. Founded in Colonial days as a companion village to adjacent Queenstown, which was adjacent to Kingstown—and on the other side toward the capital, Trenton, lay Maidenhead (now Lawrenceville).

The College of New Jersey (now Princeton University) was founded in 1746 in Princetown, after Harvard, William & Mary, and Yale. Both the town and collage figured prominently in the Revolution; for a short time the Continental Congress had to use Nassau Hall, the college's single building, after being chased by the British out of Philadelphia. During the Battle of Princeton on January 2, 1777, General George Washington capped his brilliant Christmas counter-offensive across the icy Delaware River, capturing Trenton and then by besting the Brits within sight of Nassau Hall.

In that very Nassau Hall, the exterior very much like it has always been, at graduation I received my commission as a Second Lieutenant in the U.S. Marine Corps Reserve, under the famous portrait of Washington at that battle, painted by Washington's aide, artist Colonel Charles Willson Peale.

> DIGRESSION: Incurable 'Romantic' that I was—*still am*—I followed what I thought was the English model, that is, that 'every University man owed it to his country to serve as an officer in its military', bringing his erudition, intellect, and leadership qualities to that élite Officer Corps. The movies helped instill that idea as did most of the war reporting to this naïve receptor. My combat experiences in the Korean War affirmed some of that notion and deflated some; in the modern world it takes all kinds. But, from such discernment, I decided not to 'go regular' and make the Marine Corps a career; I did stay in the active Reserve for 30 years, though, attaining colonelcy and retirement with a pension.
>
> My mentor, Brigadier General Edwin H. Simmons, however, did epitomize that idealized officer: tall, commanding, charismatic, erudite, brave, decorated in combat in three wars, and a noted writer and historian as well. I never met another quite like him.
>
> As for my tangential Marine Reserve career, I kept my infantry rating, earned public affairs' and photo officer's as well, attended Amphibious Warfare and Command & Staff schools, including the Naval War college, attained the rank of colonel at age forty, became a combat artist, with a hundred sketches and paintings in the Marine Corps Museum collection and the Pentagon, as well as

historian with one of the most praised illustrated volumes on the Corps. I was awarded the prestigious Legion of Merit for my heading the Marine combat art team in the Gulf War, in which I drove a Jeep Cherokee right behind the assaulting elements into Kuwait City.

There is little doubt that my military training at Bolles school had a lot to do with my successful Marine Reserve career, which was an active sideline to my main Madison Avenue, television, art, and writing ones.

Current Heart throb, Heather Roulston of New York and Briarcliff College after that great event. "She was the ONE," I thought, but the Korean War interrupted things.

Graduation: June 15, 1950

An hour later, I was in cap and gown grouped with my Class of 1950, seated in rows of chairs on the lawn in front of Nassau Hall waiting to receive my diploma. Rascals that we were, a couple of classmates and I had flasks of martinis (ugh! in pewter, yet!) inside our coat pockets with a flexible tube running up to our mouths so we could daringly sip through the ceremony. If the reader doesn't know already —and neither do most of the parents of graduating students—the Valedictory speech is always given in Latin, which impresses the audience. The joke is, however, that each graduating senior is handed a cue sheet to follow along, and at appropriate points, instructions are written: *Hic applaudit...hic gemuset...hic* (whatever the Latin word for 'cheer' is), and so forth—to the total amazement of parents and friends alike.

At Spring graduation time, the Princeton campus is a contained carnival called "Reunions," where each class of the past has a large tent with limitless quantities of beer and live band entertainment...festivities that go long into the night and culminate that Saturday with an enormous "P-Rade" of alumni (and now, alumnae) in various Orange and Black attire (for the older classes, sport coats, as depicted here). The event is unequalled on any campus anywhere.

From a series of acrylic paintings I did of campus life in the late 1970s, now in the University's collection.

The "Honor System"

The one thing that stood out above all else at both Sewanee and Princeton was the Honor Code. When I attended both, the system worked. That could have been the type of generation we were: the no-frill '30s and '40s, or the signs of those times, *Good* just having won over *Evil* in the world-wide conflagration—or the euphoria that came with Peace—despite the advent of the atomic age and the Cold War.

Whatever the underlying cause, a student's honesty and integrity were at stake and back in that era that meant something.

I never saw any attempts at cheating and it was certainly not in my own character to do so. I must admit, though, that was a bit to my detriment in my later life when *Integrity* met *street smarts*—and, in all walks of life. In my naïvety from a pretty sheltered life in a prep school, to élite institutions of learning, and even in the Marine Corps, where I was set apart as an officer, I found it hard to believe that other people did not think or act as I did. In short, when my 'honor' met 'street smarts', I often did not know what hit me. When I took total responsibility for the success or failure of a project, I had to find out the hard way a basic truth that when it was a success, everyone shared in the spoils; but, when it was not, I was left alone. That did not matter to me as I was a leader and charged onward. It was the surreptitious undercutting that I was oblivious of that hurt. As a leader, not a follower, I stood my ground when the followers covered their butts. Thus, I lost many a battle without ever knowing there had been a fight.

In those saner days before the so-called "Hippie Revolution" of the late 1960s, the Princeton campus was a safe and tranquil place. The campus *police*—if they could really be called that—consisted of four plain-clothes Proctors who used avuncular persuasion instead of hand-cuffs. They would deal with rowdiness, inebriation, and quelling minor disturbances, not by being confrontational—to the contrary—by being conciliatory and thus were highly respected by the student body.

Today, there is a small force of uniformed police on campus, with vehicles, two-way radios—no doubt iPhones, stun guns, and who knows what else? There are occasional muggings and even rapes on campuses at major colleges and universities and many of both sexes are advised to walk in twos at night. From the innocent clatter of restless students breaking the nighttime calm, there are now rampant demonstrations and nude streakings—not to mention 'binge drinking'. Oh, we did a lot of boozing in my day—and I joined those once or twice who swilled far too much—but it was not rampant. Today's vices, prompted by sky-high tuition fees puts pressure on grades and the coercion of faculty who try to maintain grade integrity, plus non-sensical social media absorption and a lack of manners and respect—compounded by an almost universal the drug culture—I am glad my undergraduate days are far behind me. (Yes, I read *I Am Charlotte Simmons*). I feel for those who come to college without proper high schooling, as well, and who manage to get some sort of certificate (call it a diploma) and find that the world is not greeting them with open arms. Especially in the dismal condition of the present economy.

In my humble opinion, I would imagine Sewanee continues to live up to its tradition of an Honor System (being an Episcopal institution); but I have my doubts about Princeton. Oh, there will be a hue and cry over this statement and defensive retorts, but the later generations of students are not what they were decades ago. Despite the fact that today's may be cited as smarter and more in keeping with evolving technology, I have my doubts that they will make for a better world.

The digital and the internet ages may afford far greater things than my generation ever dreamed of, but something that we had—perhaps it was a better grasp on reality—has been lost. Due to mass media in this overwhelming information age, who can possibly keep up with plagiarism, cheating, deceit, stealing, and other crimes when it is shown constantly in media coming from the high places that are supposed to be our models? Yes, I know it has always been thus, but to have the media expose it constantly tends to make one cynical and turn inward. The anonymity that erodes this internet age has become a devil-like monster that breeds a liberal-humanism that has almost completely replaced our heretofore Judeo-Christian core.

We've come a long way, Baby—but have we really?

A fitting end to the 1940s?

Depends: I had not given one twit of thought as to what I would do after graduation. Go to Paris? Paint? How? Where would the money come from? How would I support myself?

As good fortune would have it, my grandparents were to take a cruise out of New York and wanted to drive up and leave their big Packard with me, if I would agree to stay at Princeton for another two weeks—*couldn't turn that down*! They must have given me some gas and living money. I parked myself right over in one of the rooms at my Key & Seal club.

Driving around leisurely one day out toward New Hope, Pennsylvania, as I crossed a quaint little stone bridge, I noticed a lovely girl sitting on the wall—just waiting for me to stop, turn around, and greet her. Which, in my best Princetonian manner I quickly did. It was unbelievable! Her name was Cloe Stewart and she was gorgeous, turned out to have just graduated from high school, and her father was a noted magazine illustrator. We went to her house forthwith and I was introduced to him and her mother. Fascinating people—as was she.

What could have been better? I had just acquired a date for the whole two weeks, although I don't know how I handled paying for taking her to lunch or dinner. Anyway, I drew a beautiful pencil portrait of her, which impressed her father—to my great pleasure.

The beautiful "damsel by the bridge," Cloe Stewart, who posed for my pencil sketch just after graduation in June of 1950 in Princeton.

My first job opportunity:

Then, I got wind that the principal of the Princeton High School conducted a summer camp for privileged kids up at a place just north of New York city near Carmel, called The Gypsy Trail Club. This coincided with the return of my grandparents, so I availed myself, and off I went.

The Gypsy Trail was a marvelous compound of cottages tucked in the woods, a clubhouse, and a dock on a large lake. We camp counselors, all college students or grads, were treated, not as the employees, but as staff and thus were free to mingle with the residents. Besides—how opportune!—my then girlfriend whom I had invited to Princeton weekends and to my graduation, Heather Roulston, who lived in NYC and had graduated from Briarcliff College at Briarcliff Manor, was there, too, in her parents' cottage.

This is too long a story to continue, so let it be summarized that, in addition to my absolutely adoring the little five-to-six year olds we supervised, there was my love (at the time) to be with after hours. Like many a fairy-tale love story, however, during the latter part of the six-week session, another beauty, Judi Mitchell, whose family also had a cottage there, began to usurp my interest. *Oh, callous youth!*

The upshot is that, when I returned from the Korean War, we all went our separate ways, and over the years all three of us have kept in touch and have met once or twice.

My next—quite different—job:

When the delightful summer session was over, I already had my next job awaiting. During the time, on June 25, the war in Korea erupted, and as a newly-minted Marine second lieutenant, I was notified that my orders to active duty would come the first of September, a month away.

All that might be in my next book; but this marks the end of this one.

Postlude

The "examined" life:

Although ancient Greek philosopher Socrates is cited (by Plato) as having said: "The unexamined life is not worth living" and many have added the rejoinder: "...but the un-lived life in not worth examining," I have always been aware of the kind of life I have lived and have been examining it as I lived it. Don't we all do that?—at least to some extent?

As you can conclude from the foregoing, my formative years were filled with unmitigated happiness; yes, I was a privileged kid. That wasn't my doing, it was my good fortune. One might rightly observe that I was spoiled, and I guess I was. However, I was not a little brat about it or a conceited little a-hole. My parents and grandparents brought me up with no trouble from me; I was inquisitive, gregarious, contented, and obedient (*thrifty, brave, clean and reverent—like a good Boy Scout*). No one taught me particularly any so-called work ethic; when the time came for me to work—like after college—I went right to it—and to this day, I still *work* constantly in retirement at my writing and art.

Blessed—or *cursed*—with talent, I have switched jobs many times in my sixty-five year career, if one can call it that. Following the Korean War, in which at age 22 I led 85 battle-hardened Marines in combat against North Korean and Chinese enemy (which I've pointed out was pretty good for an 'Art Major'), I chose (as I mentioned previously) to stay with the Marine Reserves, which oddly became the backbone of my adult life of job changes, about which my dear Mother always nagged me: "Avery, why can't you keep a job?" She, being from a generation and social stratum that was always traditional, secure, and one-dimensional, could not comprehend my seeking new challenges, rather than atrophying in one place and getting a crummy gold watch when I retired on Social Security. (I actually acted on a similar concept when I was on the faculty of the School of Journalism and Communications at the University of Florida after receiving my MFA in 1956: I overheard a remark that caused me immediately to return to television broadcasting. A retiring professor was bragging that, after 30 years of teaching, he was about to receive his annual retirement: $6,000 a year! I had been making more than that as a local TV director before moving to Gainesville to earn my MFA!)

I then said to myself—"This ain't for me!" and went back to television as the Operations director of a large mid-western NBC affiliate station, WSAZ-TV, and later to New York and other ventures.

The old truism had also struck me after three years of teaching that,

"Those who *CAN*—Do; those who *CAN'T*—Teach."

So, in essence, I have to conclude that the 1930s and '40s were, for me at least—perhaps not for others—the best formative decades I could ever have wished for. By good fortune throughout life, I have been spared personal tragedies but not criticisms for failures and shortcomings—but not for those critical shortcomings that only I knew I did not live up to. I discovered, though, that I had a particular strength when faced with adversity—and, though not Jewish, a good dose of *chutzpah*.

No, I would never want to go back to them. I am content to leave them in the past and express here some small tribute to them and the wonderful people who touched my life during those years.

This was *my* early life, and I wouldn't have traded it for anyone else's—nor would I in any case want to relive them.

The following six adult and career decades were still more exciting and fulfilling: marriage to that tall Jacksonville girl, Kitty Adams (B.A. Vanderbilt) and our three sons (writer, Avery, Jr [Vassar/Johns Hopkins/U.VA.], architect, Richard [Vanderbilt & U.VA], and musician, Matthew [Harvard/Berkely Music Sch.]) and a daughter, lawyer-photographer, Isabel [Vassar & Wm. & Mary LLD]). Career-wise: my teaching, television (both local and national), three top advertising agencies (Campbell-Ewald, Manoff, Wm. Esty) on Madison Avenue in NYC as a TV art director-producer; my own advertising-media company (Ivy International)—divorce—an abortive attempt at Evangelism—a new marriage (Lise Dickerson [U. of Montreal]), new jobs in real estate, stockbrokering, prep school teaching, and personal ventures: magazine publishing, portrait painting, and writing (*Art of War* and *Semper Fi: the Definitive Illustrated History of the U.S. Marines,* both published by Barnes & Noble NY in 2002 and 2005-10).

Not to be overlooked: two additional wars in combat in the Marine Corps: Vietnam as a LtCol, combat artist; and the Gulf War as colonel, head Marine Combat Artist, for which I was awarded the Legion of Merit.

So, let this book be a part of the self-examination; the remainder is still a work in-progress.

...Now: *At my back I always hear...Time's wingèd chariot drawing near...and yonder all before us lie...deserts of vast eternity....*

Ok. Corny. But I have lived with those lines all my adult life. They give me more comfort than any others.

Youthful Dreamer

Aging Realist

Horace Avery Chenoweth, Sr.
2014

www.ingramcontent.com/pod-product-compliance
Lightning Source LLC
LaVergne TN
LVHW081352060426
835510LV00013B/1788